TOWARDS A CRITICAL SOCIOLOGY

By the same author
CULTURE AS PRAXIS

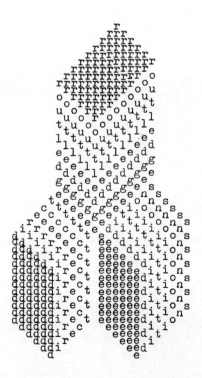

# TOWARDS A CRITICAL SOCIOLOGY
## An essay on commonsense and emancipation

ZYGMUNT BAUMAN

If a decent society has been a possibility for
at least a very long time, the real problem
becomes to explain why humanity did not or
perhaps could not want one
Barrington Moore, Jr

ROUTLEDGE DIRECT EDITIONS

ROUTLEDGE & KEGAN PAUL
London and Boston

First published in 1976
by Routledge & Kegan Paul Ltd
Broadway House, 68-74 Carter Lane,
London EC4V 5EL and
9 Park Street,
Boston, Mass. 02108, USA
Manuscript typed by Pam Pope
Printed and bound in Great Britain
by Unwin Brothers Limited,
The Gresham Press, Old Woking, Surrey
A member of the Staples Printing Group
© Zygmunt Bauman 1976

ISBN 0 7100 8306 8

# CONTENTS

# Chapter 1

# THE SCIENCE OF UNFREEDOM

'SECOND NATURE' DEFINED

Whatever may be currently said about the form sociology ought to take, sociology as we know it (and as it has been known ever since it was given this name) was born of the discovery of the 'second nature'.

'Nature' is a cultural concept. It stands for that irremovable component of human experience which defies human will and sets un-encroachable limits to human action. Nature is, therefore, a by-product of the thrust for freedom. Only when men set out self-consciously to make their condition different from what they exper-ience, do they need a name to connote the resistance they encounter. In this sense nature, as a concept, is a product of human practice which transcends the routine and the habitual, and sails on to un-charted waters, guided by an image of what-is-not-yet-but-ought-to-be.

The realm of unfreedom is the only immutable meaning of 'nature' which is rooted in human experience. All other features predicated upon the concept are once, or more than once, removed from the 'directly given', being outcomes of the theoretical processing of elementary experience. For instance, nature is the opposite of culture, in so far as culture is the sphere of human creativity and design; nature is inhuman, in so far as 'being human' includes setting goals and ideal standards; nature is meaningless, in so far as bestowing meanings is an act of will and the constitution of free-dom; nature is determined, in so far as freedom consists in leaving determination behind.

Neither the images nor models of nature prevalent at any given time can be considered necessary attributes of the concept. The 'thematic content' of the concept (as Gerald Holton would put it) (1) has changed in the last century almost beyond recognition. The intrinsic order and harmony of the law-abiding cosmos has been re-placed by an impenetrable labyrinth which, only thanks to the scient-ist's chalk marks, becomes passable; discovery of the 'objective order' has been replaced by the imposition of intelligible order upon meaningless diversity. The one element which has survived, and, indeed, has emerged unscathed from all these ontological revolutions, is the experience of constraint effectively placed on human action and imagery.  And this is, perhaps, the only 'essence' of nature, pared to the bones of theoretically unprocessed pristine experience.

There is, however, yet another sense in which nature can be conceived as a by-product of human practice.  Nature is given to human experience as the only medium upon which human action is turned.  It is present in human action from its very beginning, from its very conception as a design of a form yet to be objectified by action; nature is what mediates between the ideal design and its objectified replica.  Human action would not be possible but for the presence of nature.  Nature is experienced as much as the locus, as it is perceived as the ultimate limit of human action.  Men experience nature in the same dual, equivocal way in which the sculptor encounters his formless lump of stone:  it lies in front of him, compliant and inviting, waiting to absorb and to incarnate his creative ideas - but its willingness to oblige is highly selective;  in fact, the stone has made its own choice well before the sculptor grasps his chisel.  The stone, one could say, has classified the sculptor's ideas into attainable and unattainable, reasonable and foolish.  To be free to act, the sculptor must learn the limits of his freedom: he must learn how to read the map of his freedom charted upon the grain of the rock.

The two elements of experience which combine into the idea of nature are, in fact, in dialectical unity.  There would be no discovery of constraints were there no action guided by images which transcend these constraints;  but there would be no such action were not the human condition experienced as enclosed in such a tight frame.  The two elements condition each other;  more than that, they can present themselves to men either together or not at all. Constraint and freedom are married to each other for better or worse and their wedlock would be broken only if a return to the naive primaeval unity of man and his condition (rendering nature 'unproblematic' again) were conceivable.  On the other hand, the two elements may be, and indeed are, perceived separately and hence articulated independently, if not in opposition to each other. Undialectically, each success lends epistemological support to the notion of freedom without constraint.  Equally undialectically, every defeat lends plausibility to an idea of constraint which exists without being tested and brought into experiential relief by intractable human action.  When processed theoretically, this original error has been forged time and again into a false dilemma. The dilemma itself remains constant as the existential experience itself, though its names vary as does the cultural code.  It has been called individual and society, voluntarism and determinism, control and system, and many other names.  Whatever its names, however, it invariably leads on to the arid soil of undialectics on which the living tree of human experience can all but perish.

It is almost four centuries since Francis Bacon perceptively grasped the elusive dialectics of nature, as it appears to acting humans:  Nature is only subdued by submission.  At the time Bacon wrote these words the assumption that nature was something to be conquered the subdued did not require more arguing perhaps than other commonsensical beliefs did.  By that time, Bacon's readers

had emerged from that unproblematic 'unity of living and active
humanity with the natural, inorganic conditions of their metabolic
exchange with nature, and hence their appropriation of nature', which
'did not require explanation', as it was not a result of 'a historic
process', (2) they had already found themselves, as a result of the
history of their own making (though not of their own knowledge), face
to face with the conditions of their metabolism, confronting them as
'something alien and objective'. (2) They had already set themselves individual goals which transcended their social conditions,
and hence put the flexibility of those conditions to the test; in
the process, they discovered this stubborn and stiff resistance from
which they coined the image of Nature as an active, self-governing
and self-sustained partner of their condition. Thus nature came to
be 'directly given' in their experience. Bacon's was the resigned
admission that nature was there to stay, and that its presence was
not to be put in question. The conditions which made for this
presence – the situation in which the individual makes his way
through the social world alone, left to himself and forced into
autonomy – were neither penetrated, nor considered problematic.
Bacon combined a call to surrender with advice on how to make the
best of the situation which followed it. He suggested that serfdom
could be turned into mastery; and knowledge was assigned the role
of the magic wand which would accomplish the transformation. The
structure of the stone is not of the sculptor's making; he can still
make the stone accept his intentions, but only by learning what the
stone will not accept. One has only to extend this metaphor so as
to embrace the totality of the human condition. Life then becomes
the art of the possible, and knowledge is there to teach us how to
distinguish the possible from idle dreams.

Since Bacon at least, knowledge has presided over the process of
mediation between freedom and the limitations of human action. The
most prestigious kind of knowledge of all (sometimes, indeed, portrayed as the only valid knowledge), science, has established itself
in our culture as the study of the limits of human freedom, pursued
in order to enhance the exploitation of the remaining field of
action. Indeed, science has been constituted more by the elimination of the impossible, the suppression of the unrealistic, the
exclusion of the morbid questions, than by the variegated and changing content of its positive preoccupations. Science, as we know it,
can be defined as knowledge of unfreedom.

Hegel's celebrated definition of freedom as comprehended necessity
aptly epitomized the subtle evolution of Bacon's idea in the process
of its absorption by commonsensical lore. To be free means to know
one's potentiality; knowing potentiality is a negative knowledge,
i.e. knowledge of what one is prevented from doing. Proper knowledge can assure that a man will never experience his constraints as
oppression; it is the unknown, unsuspected necessity which is confronted as suffering, frustration, and humiliating defeat. But it
is only unenlightened action which exposes necessity as an alien,
hostile, and thoroughly negative force. An informed action, on the
contrary, needs necessity as its positive foundation. A genuinely
free action would not be possible were there no necessity: free
action means reaching one's ends by a chain of appropriate acts; but
it is the necessary laws connecting acts with their effects, which

make them 'appropriate' to the intended ends.   And thus the mutual
dependence between freedom and necessity has two complementary
aspects.   The negative aspect is revealed by ignorant action;  it
is most fully exposed by a blinded moth crashing against a window-
pane.   But for an informed action the necessary is no longer a
negative force;  on the contrary, it enters the action itself as an
indispensable condition of its success.   The moment it has become
calculable - known - the necessary is a positive condition  of freedom.

To Weber the necessary was the condition of rationality.   Indeed,
rational action required unfreedom for it to be possible at all.
It is the rules, which confront each individual cog in the bureaucratic machine with all the merciless, indomitable power of nature -
the rules which make the external walls of the action safely and
predictably stable - which render bureaucracy rational, which permit
the bureaucrats carefully to select means for the ends, secure in the
knowledge that the means will indeed bring forth the objectives they
wish, or are told, to achieve.   The rational action commences when
the rules are 'already there';  it does not account for the origins
of rules, explain why rules remain strong, or why they take on the
shape they possess.   The question of the origins of rules, of the
origins of the environmental necessity of bureaucratic action, cannot
be phrased in the language of rationality.   If asked, however, it
will invite an answer similar to that given to the parallel question
'why is nature there?'   It will inevitably point to the irrational
as much as the latter question points to God.   'If rationality is
embodied in administration .., legislative force must be irrational.'
(4)  Inasmuch as science eliminates questions which lead to God, the
scientifically informed action eliminates acts which lead to irrationality.   Both employ nature, or nature-like necessity, as their
lever.   The price they willingly pay for the gain in efficiency is
the agreement never to question its legitimacy.   To be sure, this
legitimacy cannot be questioned  by science, just as it cannot be
challenged by a rational action.   Both are what they are in so far
as nature remains the realm of omnipotent and unchallengeable
necessity.

Thus freedom boils down, for all practical purposes, to the
possibility of acting rationally.   It is the rational action which
embodies both the negative and the positive aspects of freedom.
Only by acting rationally can one keep painful constraints at a
safe distance, at which they can neither inflict pain not incur
wrath;  a man buttresses, simultaneously, his hopes and calculations
on the secure foundations of immutable, and so comfortingly predictable, laws.   Knowledge is the crucial factor in both aspects of
this freedom-rationality.   Knowledge means emancipation.   It trans-
forms fetters into tools of action, prison walls into horizons of
freedom, fear into curiosity, hate into love.   Knowing one's limits
means reconciliation.   There is no need to be scared now, and
nature, once feared or painful if ignored, may be enthusiastically
embraced as the house of freedom.   Thus, it is Nature, the hostess,
who sets the rules of the game, and who defines this freedom.

'Everything that can be, is' proclaimed Buffon in his 'Histoire
naturelle'.   'Opposed to nature, contrary to reason' - was
Diderot's logical conclusion in his 'Voyage de Bougainville'.   The

natural, for him, is not just the inevitable and unavoidable: it is
the appropriate, the apposite, the good, the sacred, the undefiable.
Nature supplies not just the boundaries of reasonable action and
thought: it supplies reason itself.  All valid knowledge is a reflection of nature.  The power of man consists in his ability to
'know' what he cannot do.  Science is there to teach him exactly
this.  This is the only way in which science 'is' power.

It took just one little step to cast this reflective knowledge
already established in the role of the linchpin of freedom, as the
pattern for settling human affairs.  Nature is 'a living power,
immense, which embraces everything, animates everything' - eulogized
Buffon;  including man himself - Hume added the finishing touch.
And thus we learn from the 'Treatise of Human Nature' that the only
science of man is Human Nature.  In 'An Enquiry Concerning Human
Understanding' conclusions are drawn, which amount to no less than
a unilateral declaration of independence proclaimed on behalf of
sociology, the new science to come and to crown the rapidly rising
edifice of human knowledge:  'There is a great uniformity among the
actions of men, in all nations and ages';  'human nature remains
still the same, in its principles and operations';  'Mankind are so
much the same, in all times and places, that history informs us of
nothing new or strange in this particular'.  With such stubborn,
unflinching uniformity extending over all time and all space, the
use of nature's name to describe human properties is fully warranted.
And since science is knowledge of what nature is not, a science of
man and his affairs is feasible and, indeed, necessary, if men wish
to attain freedom - both negative and positive - in determining
their own conditions.  It goes without saying that human nature,
now scientifically revealed and laid bare, will determine the boundaries and the content of this freedom.

The study of human nature, however, posed a problem which had
never been faced when non-human nature was the sole object of
inquiry.  The latter is continually at peace with itself;  it never
rebels against its own laws - its harmony and uniformity have been
pre-set and built into its very mechanism.  As Hegel would have
said, Nature (referring to non-human nature) has no history;  to wit,
it knows no individual, unique, wayward, out-of-the-ordinary events.
This view of nature found its foremost expression, as Peter Gay
recently pointed out, in the vehement passion with which the prea-
chers on behalf of the Scientific Age fought the concept of miracle.
To explain an inexplicable occurrence, Diderot 'would seek natural-
istic reasons - a practical joke, a conspiracy, or perhaps his own
madness'.  To Hume, a miracle would have been 'a violation of the
laws of nature, and such a violation is by definition impossible.
If a miracle seems to occur, it must be treated either as a mend-
acious report or as a natural event for which, at present, no
scientific explanation is available'. (5)  There was, of course,
no particular reason why this uncompromising attitude could not be
extended to embrace the totality of human deeds.  It was, in fact,
extended in such a way, but much later, in the behaviouristic idiom
of the science of man, which pushed the sober incredulity of
science in general, tested on non-human objects, to its logical
limits.  Still, the behaviouristic programme, bold and iconoclastic
as it seemed to those who drafted it and to those who opposed it

alike, was by no means an odd denizen of the castle of science.    No
behaviourist denies that human action may be irrational;  but the one
thing every behaviourist will emphatically reject is the possibility
of conduct, rational or irrational, which has no cause, i.e., which
could be different from what it was, given the conditions under which
it took place.

The only difference between human and non-human occurrences
consists, therefore, in the following:  in human affairs a dangerous
and portentous chasm tends to appear, unknown to non-human nature,
between human conduct and nature's commandments.    In the case of non-
human phenomena, nature itself, without human intervention, takes
care of the harmony between the necessary and the actual, the
identity of the real and the good;  in the human case, however, the
gap between the two must be bridged artificially, and requires sustained and conscious effort.   (Adam, we remember, was the only
creation of God, of whom He did not assert a fortiori:  it was
good ...).   As Louis de Bonald asserted in 'Théorie de l'education
sociale et de l'administration publique', 'Nature creates society,
men rule the government.   Since Nature is essentially perfect, it
creates, or intends to create, a perfect society;  since he is essentially depraved, man plays havoc with administration or tends
constantly to botch it'.   Knowledge of natural verdicts, followed
and supported by the respect for what is known, is the stuff of which
the bridge linking the actual to the necessary, the real to the good,
may and should be constructed.

In his selfishness, avarice, irrationality, foolishness, man is
as 'determined' by his own nature as he is in the most glorious
moments of the law-abiding citizen's euphoria.   The second is not,
therefore, automatically assured.   It will not become the rule unless an effort is made to tip the balance towards the laws which
Nature has fixed for the society.

And thus, for the first time, the individual's nature is pitted
against the nature of the society.   Emerging from the pre-modern
'natural unity' of man with his corporative society and thrown into
a fluid, under-determined situation which called for choice and decision, men articulated their novel experience (or had it articulated
for them) as the clash between the individual and the society.   And
so society took off on its long, and still continuing, career of the
'second nature', in which it is perceived by commonsensical wisdom as
an alien, uncompromising, demanding and high-handed power - exactly
like non-human nature.   To abide by the rules of reason, to behave
rationally, to achieve success, to be free, man now had to accommodate himself to the 'second nature' as much as he had tried to
accommodate himself to the first.   He may be still reluctant to do
this:  people do time and again refuse to be reasonable.   If it
were the law of non-human nature which was challenged by man's
default, nature itself would soon bring the delinquent into line.
If, however, it were the law fixed by nature for humans which was
defied, the task would have to be performed by humans.   'Whoever
shall refuse to obey the general will', Jean Jacques Rousseau said
in his 'Social Contract', 'must be constrained by the whole body of
his fellow citizens to do so:  which is no more than to say that it
may be necessary to compel a man to be free.'

Who, however, is to do the compelling?   And what power will lend legitimation to his act? Rousseau's answer is simultaneously pre-scientific (certainly pre-sociological) and anticipative of discoveries at which sociology will wearily arrive after a century or more of carefree, though dedicated, dalliance with the idea of an unproblematically nature-like society. Rousseau was in fact strikingly modern, by our own standards, in portraying the commanding authority of society as composed of the multitude of individual wills of 'homini socii', and in defining this authority, accordingly, as general will; it is the wording alone, not the substance, which will appear to us as archaic under closer scrutiny. He was, however, pre-scientific in pinning his hope of the ultimate reconciliation between unruly individual nature and the demands of the supra-individual entity on political action, leaving no room for the scholar, the pundit, the educator, or for that matter, for specifically scientific cognition. The one thing which really counts is the determination of the Sovereign, the Ruler, the Legislator to crush whatever resistance he may encounter on his way to 'change the very stuff of human nature; to transform each individual .... To take from a man his own proper powers, and to give him in exchange powers foreign to him as a person, which he can use only if he is helped by the rest of community'. It is still an exhortation to society to become a supreme and merciless (though benevolent) power, rather than a recognition that, indeed, it has become one, and has been one for a long time. And it is an expression of hope that the clash between human intentions and the mysterious, hostile force called society which people keep experiencing, is not, or should not be, a timeless condition; it can be explained away as a clash between 'wrong' intentions and 'badly' organized society; and such a clash, together with ensuing sufferings, may well disappear if the wrongs are done away with. 'Scientific sociology' will reject both assumptions. It will assume instead that society's being a supreme reality to men is not a matter of human, or even of super-human, choice. And it will accept that the tension between untamed human selfishness and the survival needs of the social totality (one which Blaise Pascal sought to reconcile by religious faith) is there to stay. Last but not least, having assigned to the 'second reality' the dignity of the only source of reason, it will deprive itself of the method of distinguishing between the good and the actual, slowly but surely blending the good and the real into one, until the idea of Truth as the locus of highest authority (and, for science, the only one) will declare the good off limits.

And so the ground will be swept clean for the triumphant ascent of the positive science of the social – that science which views 'society' as nature in its own right, as orderly and regular as the 'first nature' appears to the natural scientist, and legislating for human action as much as the 'first nature', thanks to the natural scientist. The post-revolutionary generation of philosophers plunged into the new faith with the relish and impetuous intolerance of new converts. It fell upon Claude de Saint-Simon to articulate the catechism of the new creed:

The supreme law of progress of the human spirit carries along and dominates everything; men are but its instruments. Although this force derives from us, it is no more in our power to withhold ourselves from its influence, or master its

action, than to change at will the primary inpulse which
makes our planet revolve around the sun.   All we can do
is to obey this law by accounting for the course it directs,
instead of being blindly pushed by it;  and, incidentally,
it is precisely in this that the great philosophic development reserved for the present era will consist. ('L'organisateur')
   The present era will be one of discovery rather than spurious in-
vention.   'Nature has suggested to men, in each period, the most
suitable form of government .... The natural course of things has
created the institutions necessary for each age of the body social'
('Psychologie sociale'). And, therefore, the most important conclusion of all:  'One does not create a system of social organization.
One perceives the new chain of ideas and interests which has been
formed, and points it out - that is all' ('L'organisateur').  Almost
a century later, aware of the tremendous explosion of social science
these ideas ignited, Emile Durkheim will ask rhetorically:
   To think scientifically - is not it to think objectively,
   that is, to divest our notions of what is exclusively
   human in them in order to make them a reflection - as accurate as possible - of things as they are?   Is it not, in a
   word, to make the human intelligence bow before facts?  (6)
   Two observations are appropriate at this point.   From the start,
the 'second nature' had been introduced to intellectual discourse not
as an historical phenomenon, a puzzle to be explained, but as an
aprioric assumption.   To express the unqualified supremacy of
society's revolutions over human will, Saint-Simon used no less
grandiose a metaphor than that of the revolutions of celestial
bodies, which at that time seemed entirely beyond the reach of human
praxis.   It had been accepted without question that their social
world confronted men the way nature does - as something they could
live with, and sometimes even turn to their advantage, but only if
they unconditionally surrendered to its command.   The intellectual
curiosity of sociologists was subsequently drawn to disclosing the
mechanism of this supremacy and assiduously recording the rules it
posits.   When human practice was brought into the focus of their
attention, sociologists kept it consistently inside the analytical
field already confined by the previously accepted premiss.   This
methodological decision contained, as we would later see, numerous
advantages.   It supplied the scholar with clear, unequivocal criteria of the normal, as distinct from the odd and irregular;  the
unproblematic as distinct from the problematic;  the realistic as
distinct from the utopian;  the functional as distinct from the disruptive or deviant;  the rational as distinct from the irrational.
In short, it supplied sociologists with the totality of analytical
concepts and models which constituted their discipline as an autonomous intellectual discourse.   Within this discipline human
practical activity was irrevocably assigned the role of dependent
variable.   On the other hand, the above-mentioned assumption offered
the practitioners of the discourse it generated a relatively wide
territory of theoretical exploration and disagreement, which has sustained the intellectual versatility of the discipline without bringing it anywhere near a disturbance of communication such as could
lead to a retrospective questioning of the initial assumption.   The
most vehement arguments rarely transgressed the boundary of legiti-

mate discussion as drawn by the 'second nature' assumption.  Sociologists quarrelled ferociously about the right answer to the question
whose propriety they rarely doubted:  what is this second nature,
which brackets, and provides a framework for, human life activity?

Second - in passing, and perhaps without noticing it - the programme sketched by Saint-Simon and later subscribed to in practice,
if not in words, by several successive generations of sociologists,
was logically founded on two acts of conflation of problems, the
identity of which is by no means self-evident, and, therefore, must
be demonstrated to be accepted.  First, it has been assumed that the
status of the 'we' or 'men' is nothing more than the status of the
'I' or 'man'.  The product of multiplication may be larger than its
factors, but it belongs to the same set of numbers as its factors;
the act of multiplication does not endow the product with attributes
which cannot be traced back and ascribed to the factors themselves.
In the later development of sociology, the powerful current of behavioural pluralism (aptly called this by Don Martindale) accepted
this idiom literally, lock, stock, and barrel.  Most 'holists',
with Durkheim as their most prominent spokesman and pattern-setter,
having anchored the 'second nature' to the 'group', hastened to emphasize that the group 'is not reducible' to its members, however
numerous they may be.  In practice, they have been willing to accede
the group's reducibility in all respects but one;  no number of individuals, however large, can stand up to the power of the group and
defy its supremacy.  In short, the 'group' is nature all right, and
its laws, even if - in some intricate way - of human making, are not
subject to human deliberate manipulation.  Both currents, therefore,
agreed to conflate the 'we' with the 'I', and consequently felt free
to reason from one to the other.  Thus Saint Simon, in a somewhat
crude version of later, subtler exercises, takes the problem of the
individual's experience of his impotence against society as being
identical to, and conjointly explicable with, the assumed impotence
of society ('men') against its own 'supreme laws of progress' ('the
group').  This something which makes us and me alike in experiencing our and my impotence, stands, in a sense, above the realm of
human - individual or collective - action.  Laws are as they are,
and to ascribe their content to somebody's intentional activity would
be equal to surreptitiously reviving magical thinking in the guise of
scholarship.  'Positive consciousness', contrary to Comte's hopes,
did not remove God from the human universe and its conditions of intelligibility.  It only gave God a new name.

On the other hand, there is a conflation of the task placed before
the student of human affairs with the alleged existential status of
man in society.  Summing up Saint-Simon's programme, Durkheim called
the scholars of the social to 'bow before facts'.  These facts, in
Durkheim's vocabulary, are moral commands, constitutive of the
'collective consciousness' of 'the group'.  But this is precisely
what any man, in Durkheim's view (and in view of most sociologists)
is doomed to do all his life.  The 'second nature' transcends human
intelligence, represented at its highest in the activity of scholars,
as uncompromisingly and relentlessly as it does the practical potential of the individual.  However faithful sociologists remain to
Kant's warning against drawing norms from facts, this is exactly
what they do in the case under discussion:  'the fact' is, that

society is to men a 'second nature', i.e., as unchallengeable and beyond their control as non-human nature is; therefore, the 'norm' for the scholar is to treat society as such, to wit, not to attempt anything other than a 'reflection - as accurate as possible - of things as they are'.   Criteria of realism and rationality are identical in both cases; scholars must succumb to the same limitations which befall all humans, whether or not they exercise their intellectual powers in reflection upon their predicament.   Thinking does not engender a qualitatively distinct situation.   If anything, it helps the 'second nature' to actualize its intrinsic tendencies more smoothly and with less suffering than otherwise would have been the case.   It makes men (us? me?) more free by reconciling them to the necessities built into their social situation.

Nobody perhaps has done more for establishing the case for 'second nature', so understood, than Auguste Comte.   The disciple of Saint-Simon plunged into the task of spelling out his teacher's implicit ideas and their consequences with a pristine enthusiasm and fearlessness which can only really be understood against the background of unknown whirlwinds and underwater reefs which obstructed the way ahead.   To Comte above all belongs the merit of singling out 'the social' as a separate, autonomous, and in a sense crucial dimension of human situation.   The idea of merciless regularity ingrained in human affairs, which transcends individual fate and is powerful enough to confound most ingenious schemes, was not new when Comte entered the debate.   At least a century before, in 'The Spirit of the Laws', Montesquieu kept asking the crucial question upon which sociology as a positive science was to be built: 'Who can be guarded against events that incessantly arise from the nature of things?'   It was clear to him, as it was to the rest of 'les philosophes', that 'amidst such an infinite diversity of laws and manners' men 'were not solely conducted by the caprice of fancy'. To be sure, the various elements of the idea of regularity, later to be set apart and analysed separately, were still intertangled in a way defying what would be, from the modern perspective, meaningful discussion.   Even if he distinguished between the problems, Montesquieu could not quite decide whether the regularity he sensed consisted in the virtual elimination of freak, inexplicable acts of unrestrained fancy - in the essential determination of all human conduct, however bizarre it may seem to an uninformed eye; or, rather, in the presence of an inexorable force of super-human logic which individuals and nations do defy time and again only to lick their wounds, if they are lucky enough not to perish as a result.   But, whatever the meaning implied, the intuitively felt regularity was situated, neatly and squarely, at the level which we would describe to-day as political action.   This led to two important consequences. First, the idiom of political action was that of an end-organized, motivated human action, set upon the achievement of specified states. Whether we describe the motives in terms of personality traits, like avarice, conceit, or envy, or in terms of objectified interests, like intended unity of nation or enhancement of its glory, the motives as such remain in the centre of our attention - simultaneously the object of investigation and the tool of explanation.   It is therefore extremely difficult to divest the discussion of political phenomena of the concept of will, intentions, goals - which, to be conceived of as regular in a way transcending individual idiosyncrasy, have to be referred to phenomena located somewhere beyond the political sphere proper.   Second, it follows from the foregoing remarks that in so far as the perception of human affairs remains squashed into the idiom of political action, the naming of regularities presents well-nigh insuperable obstacles.   Historical analogy, examples from which to draw lessons, were in fact the closest approximation to the idea of regularity the pre-sociological discussion of human affairs ever reached.   It attained its unsurpassable heights in the work of Machiavelli, with the vision of history as a game whose outcome is essentially undetermined in advance; a game, however, in which some stratagems are 'truer to the logic of the situation' than others and therefore can and should be scrupulously learnt and applied by all who wish to master necessity.   The repeatability of historical occurrences was thereby translated as the perpetual efficacy of specific moves which, however, could still be employed at will.   Within the political idiom, considered in isolation from the further reaches of the human situation, the game model is perhaps the closest conceivable approximation of the idea of implanted, 'objectified' regularity.   Any further development of the idea requires the introduction of additional analytical dimensions.

It fell to Comte to trigger off the long, still unfinished process of 'peeling the onion' of the human predicament in search of the situs of the 'second nature'.   As Ronald Fletcher recently aptly observed:

> Comte was not opposed to constitution-making or to the
> clarification of moral ideals, but he believed that many
> more dimensions were active in society - practical economic
> activities, property formation, conflicts of class interests,
> scientific investigation, changes in religious belief and
> behaviour, etc. - and that only with a sound knowledge of all
> these social processes could statesmanship be sound.   For
> him, therefore, a sufficient study of 'political orders' had
> to be a thorough study of social systems.   (7)

Comte postulated the 'second layer' beneath the surface of political events:   the 'second nature' extends below the level of political history, to which the eyes of his predecessors had been fixed.   To it belongs the 'social' level, the locus of regularity and permanence hidden behind the apparently random series of political happenings. The choice, still shunned or unnoticed by the generation of Montesquieu, was finally made:   this concealed 'social nature' comes to the surface, enters the realm of human conduct not necessarily as a behaviour-determining factor (individual acts may well be, for all the scholar should care, 'undetermined' in the sense of being caused by factors unfit for scientific, always law-seeking, treatment), but as the ultimate limitation of all human freedom of action and the supreme judge of 'realism', i.e., the viability, of all human intentions.   The 'social nature' is simply that supreme force which will always gain the upper hand however viciously individual humans or human groups attempt to get the better of it.

The whole of Comte's work can be interpreted as a consistent attempt to establish the case for a 'social nature' which makes its way through the fits and starts of political history, and for social scientists as the sole interpreters of this nature and, therefore, the indispensable messengers of its commands. Comte conceived of human deeds as links in the 'great chain of being', which begins with the blind and automatic unravelling of natural forces. Only some human actions can indeed attach themselves to this chain, and the condition of doing so is their conformity to 'natural trends'; wayward, off-the-mark, refractory acts will inevitably end at the graveyard of abortive, misconceived or ignorant ventures into the realm of the impossible. Comte urged that we consider 'the artificial and voluntary order as a prolongation of the natural and involuntary order towards which all human societies naturally tend in all their aspects, so that every truly rational political institution, if it is to have real and lasting social efficiency, must rest on a preliminary exact analysis of the natural tendencies which alone can furnish its authority with firm roots; in a word, order is to be considered as something to be projected, not created, for this would be impossible'. Men may create their artificial order only if they comprehend the natural one (the alternative would be, presumably, the costly and painful method of trial and error) - they are, in a truly Hegelian fashion, free when knowing and accepting the necessary. Otherwise they are in for bitter frustration:

> The principle of the limitation of political action establishes the only true and exact point of contact between social theory and social practice ... Political intervention can effect nothing either for order or for progress except by basing itself on the tendencies of the political life of organism, so as to assist by well-chosen means its spontaneous development. (8)

This view was indeed part and parcel, if not the most prominent distinctive feature, of the genuine 'Zeitgeist', shared across the board by thinkers of all shades of political denomination. In his usual caustic and succint style, Joseph de Maistre declared in his 'Quatre Chapitres sur la Russie', that 'what is called Nature is what one cannot oppose without risking his own perdition'. While Louis de Bonald chimed in: 'Sooner or later Nature will claim its possession' ('Théorie du pouvoir politique et religieux dans la société civile'). What Comte contributed on his own, besides obsessively and repetitively harping on the motif with which everybody else at the time concerned themselves, was pinpointing this 'Nature', whose defiance equals perdition, as a supra-individual 'Spiritual Power' with a developmental logic of its own: 'Temporal power cannot be replaced by a power of a different nature without an analogous transformation in the spiritual power, and vice versa'. (9)

Comte was too preoccupied with the task of demonstrating that the 'second nature' is to be reckoned with when facile schemes of transforming human life by promulgating new laws or putting new men in power are contemplated, that he had no time nor intention to venture very far beyond this vague 'spiritual power'. To Comte, this was a simple notion, hardly requiring any further elaboration or refinement. The spectacular successes of scientific discovery of the time seemed to the members of the intellectual micro-community cogent and powerful enough a force to blaze new trials for mankind as a whole, and hence 'spiritual power' looked capable of reaching directly into the conditions of social life. The very process of 'reaching' did

not concern Comte as a difficult problem in its own right.   Perhaps
Comte was still a faithful disciple of the Enlightenment, to which he
time and again angrily reacted and whose reckless reformatory zeal
he was so keen to castigate:  he still saw the drama of human progress
as the struggle of knowledge against ignorance, truth against prejudice.    Truth, once promulgated, would easily hold its own, just
as, in its absence, the false, vitiated images of the world preached
by established churches had dominated the social fabric.   This view,
as it were, squared well with the other motif of Comte's writing -
establishing 'savants' in the role of the new spiritual leaders of
sociology, to take over social power (as distinct from the secondary
political power) from the shaking hands of the clergy who had out-
lived their theological age.   Of the approaching 'positive' era of
human history Comte wrote:

> Scientific men can alone construct this system, since it
> must flow from their positive knowledge of the relations
> that subsist between the external world and man.   This
> great operation is indispensable in order to constitute the
> class of engineers into a distinct corporation, serving as
> a permanent and regular communication between the Savants
> and Industrialists in reference to all special works.

A better, truer, more efficient knowledge will defeat and chase away
its less perfect versions as easily as a harder rock will bruise and
cut a softer one.   'When experience has at last convinced society
that the only road to riches lies through peaceful activity, or works
of industry, the direction of affairs properly passes to the industrial capacity'.   The accolade of 'savants' will be a simple natural
consequence of the new heights attained by the 'social spirit':

> When politics shall have taken the rank of a positive
> science, the public should and must accord to publicists
> the same confidence in their department, which it now
> concedes to astronomers in astronomy, to physicians in
> medicine, etc.;  with the difference however that the
> public will be exclusively entitled to point out the end
> and the aim of the work.   (10)

In this respect as well Comte was a loyal heir to the Enlightenment.   Pascal's 'homo duplex' - the selfish beast tamed and held at
bay by a super-human power - was very much an axiom to 'les philosophes', who never neglected an opportunity to manifest their disdain
for the ignorant, mentally inept masses.   However self-propelling a
truth may be when proclaimed, its discovery is an elitarian matter.
The passion-ridden, myopic, egostic multitude cannot approach the
truth unhelped.   To lay bare blinkering human passions one must
first relinquish one's own (remember Durkheim's 'divesting our
notions of what is exclusively human in them') and purify oneself of
crippling loyalties.   It takes super-human power to catch a glimpse
of the Truth.   Rousseau sketched its essential marks:

> In order to discover what social regulations are best suited
> to nations, there is needed a superior intelligence which
> can survey all the passions of mankind, though itself ex-
> posed to none:  an intelligence having no contact with our
> nature, yet knowing it to the full:  an intelligence, the
> well-being of which is independent of our own, yet willing
> to be concerned with it.   (11)

These words were intended by Rousseau as a description of God. Imperceptibly, 'savants' slipped into the mould carved for the Supreme Being. Purification of passions has always been a vital component of any rite of consecration. To approach the Absolute, humans were expected to wash away the earthly dust which covered their bodies and their souls. 'Renouncing contact with one's nature' had sacred significance and hallowing potential. By putting them in the position of supreme judges, hovering high above the vale of morbid passion, Comte consecrated 'savants'.

## 'SECOND NATURE' DEIFIED

It was left to Durkheim to deify society.    Durkheim picked up the task where Comte abandoned it.   While accepting in full, as proven, that 'spiritual power' is indeed the 'second nature' people experience as the limits of their freedom, Durkheim proceeded to ask - and possibly to answer - the question Comte had not considered puzzling or worth asking: what is the 'substance' of the 'second nature' and why is its hold on human conduct so effective?

Durkheim's ideas of social reality were begotten in the conditions of rapid though thorough secularization of French social and political life, with both the sway of institutionalized religion and the powerful 'imperial' legitimation of state power petering out and loosing their grip.   The question of how society can survive, as an integrated and solidary unit, without its traditional adhesive, became both perplexing and topical.   To restore shattered self-confidence by discovering a new cogent answer to the 'quod iuris' of national society became, so to speak, the patriotic order of the day. It was Durkheim who most earnestly answered the challenge.

On the face of it, Durkheim stripped bare and exposed the 'social nature of God', having shown that in all times, even in the most devoutly religious eras, God was nothing more than society in disguise, society's commands made sacred and therefore awe-inspiring and fearsome.   Therefore, the disappearance of God and his quiverful of thunderbolts may be considered as a minor irritant.   Society will eventually emerge unscathed from the supposed disaster - if anything, rejuvenated and reinforced, being able to confront its members undisguised and to pass its sentences in its own name.   But when viewed from another perspective - that of the ground on which the artlessly secular commands of human society may be obeyed with the same compliance and self-abandonment as the holy orders used to be - the same reasoning appears in a different light.   Instead of secularizing God, Durkheim deified society.   Time and again Durkheim sees and admits the truth: 'Kant postulates God, since without this hypothesis morality is unintelligible.   We postulate a society specifically distinct from individuals, since otherwise morality has no object and duty no roots.' (12)   To Durkheim, 'between God and society lies the choice.'   Since the choice has to be made if morality-bound social order is to be salvaged from the wreckage of religious rule, 'I see in the Divinity only society transfigured and symbolically expressed.'   On the other end of the communication channel, however, the message somewhat modifies its content: it is not necessary to call society factitious names; it may and should

be divined under its own name.   The will of the society is sufficient 'ratio' for moral commandments, and the same respect and
obedience society has always received, though in a ritual mask, is
now due to it in the same measure when it stares at us bare-faced.

In fact, though Durkheim's description of the 'second nature' is
incomparably richer and more dense than Comte's, it does not go
strikingly far beyond the Christian, and particularly Jewish theological predication of God.   Society is what 'imposes itself from
without upon the individual'; what imposes itself with 'irresistible force'; what 'surpasses the individual'; what is 'good and
desirable for the individual who cannot exist without it or deny it
without denying himself'; what is 'a personality qualitatively different from the individual personalities of which it is composed';
what is 'the authority which demands to be respected even by reason.
We feel that it dominates not only our sensitivity, but the whole of
our nature, even our rational nature.'   Durkheim's society shares
with the God of theologians its negative predication (more powerful
than men, infallible unlike men, good unlike mean individuals, etc.)
and its specific 'underdetermination':   characteristic resistance to
the attribution of traits which could lend Him, or it, a measure
of sensual tangibility.   Occasionally, Durkheim indulges in what
can be considered only as genuine theological style, thus confirming,
though in a paradoxical way, that God and his society differ in names
only:

> Society commands us because it is exterior and superior to
> us;   the moral distance between it and us makes it an
> authority before which our will defers.   But as, on the
> other hand, it is within us and 'is' us, we love and desire
> it, albeit with a 'sui generis' desire since, whatever we do,
> society can never be ours in more than a part and dominates
> us infinitely ....   If you analyse man's constitution you
> will find no trace of this sacredness with which he is in-
> vested ....   This character has been added to him by society.

And, finally, with a truly mystical self-abandonment:

> The individual submits to society and this submission is the
> condition of his liberation ....   By putting himself under
> the wing of society, he makes himself also, to a certain
> extent, dependent upon it.   But this is a liberating
> experience.   (13)

There is all the difference one can conceive of between the sob-
riety of Durkheim and the religious fervour of Pascal, Durkheim's
occasional sallies into sanctimony notwithstanding.   But, on the
whole Durkheim's work may be considered as an attempt to re-phrase
the old Pascal dilemma of 'homo duplex' in times when the grip of the
Church over human minds was rapidly failing in strength.   Or,
rather, to foreclose for the 'secular' society the passion-ridden
idiom heretofore usurped by theology.   Pascal's dilemma in fact
inspires and informs the totality of Durkheim's explorations.   Indeed, some of Durkheim's notoriously elusive suggestions (including
the most irritating of all, 'l'âme', 'mentalité', or 'conscience
collective') seem bizarre only if considered outside the context of
the continuous Pascalian tradition in French intellectual life.
There are, we are told by Pascal, two inviolable constant truths:

> One is that man in the state of his creation, or in the

state of grace, is exalted above the whole of nature, made
like unto God and sharing in His divinity.   The other is that
in the state of corruption and sin he has fallen from that
first state and has become like the beasts... Let us then
conceive that man's condition is dual.   Let us conceive that
man infinitely transcends man, and that without the aid of
faith he would remain inconceivable to himself, for who
cannot see that unless we realize the duality of human nature
we remain invincibly ignorant of the truth about ourselves.
To escape from this duality of existence, the source of permanent
sufferings and the tormenting clash between beastly instincts and
moral conscience, one has to embrace God - one has, in fact, to
surrender, willingly and zealously, to His divine grace.

True conversion consists in self-annihilation before the universal
being whom we have so often vexed and who is perfectly entitled to
destroy us at any moment, in recognizing that we can do nothing
without Him and that we have deserved nothing but His disfavour...
He that is joined to the Lord is one spirit, we love ourselves
because we are members of Christ.   We love Christ because he is
the body of which we are members.   All are one.   One is in the
other ....   (14)

Durkheim will 'secularize' Pascal: 'To love society is to love both
something beyond us and something in ourselves.   We could not wish
to be free of society without wishing to finish our existence as
men.' (15)  In Pascal, society was personified.   In Durkheim, it
has been reified.   In both cases it has remained deified.

The concept of society was introduced by Durkheim almost on the
strength of definition.   With his essence torn apart into bits he
cannot reconcile on his own, man becomes humanized only when he
surrenders to society.   There is, in fact, no way to define 'being
human' other than by referring back to the definition currently
imposed by a given society.   A statement 'this is a bad society' is
inexpressible within Durkheimian logic;   society may be inefficient,
poorly organized, as happens in the case of 'anomie' - the failure of
society to get its message through or to supply goods made desirable
by its norms.   But society cannot be bad;   how could it be, if it
is the only foundation, measure, and authority behind morality, the
knowledge of good and evil.   'It is impossible to desire a morality
other than that endorsed by the condition of society at a given time.
To desire a morality other than that implied by the nature of society
is to deny the latter and, consequently, oneself'.   There is no
detached, independent scale of values with which the morality sanct-
ioned by a given society can be gauged and evaluated, and thus there
is no logic in which the sentence 'this society is bad' would make
sense.   Man, therefore, can be a moral being only as a result of
his obedience to his society.   Social conformity and humanity
conflate.

The alternative is not a 'better society' (this would be meaningless), but devolution to animal life.

Imagine a being liberated from all external restraint, a
despot still more absolute than those of which history
tells us, a despot that no external power can restrain or
influence.   By definition, the desires of such a being
are irresistible.   Shall we say, then, that he is all-

powerful?   Certainly not, since he himself cannot resist
his desires.   They are masters of him, as of everything
else.   He submits to them; he does not dominate them.
And so the choice is between two kinds of unfreedom:   the beastly and
the human one.   This is the meaning of the 'liberating surrender' to
the domination of the society.   Surrendering, men sacrifice only
their inferior, animal freedom, the corrupt part - as Pascal would
say - of their personality.   Instead, they are given the opportunity
to display their human side in the only available form of humanity,
as forged by the particular group from which it is acquired.
Now, becoming human is not necessarily an inherent desire of men.
At any rate, it is too serious a business to be left to the free
choice of individuals.   As Rousseau would say, men 'must be forced
to be human.'   In Durkheim's words, 'society can neither create
itself nor recreate itself without at the same time creating an
ideal.'   While man 'could not be a social being, that is to say, he
could not be a man, if he had not acquired' it.   (16)   Society, which
- being coterminous with morality - is the good incarnate, and simultaneously the supreme judge of it, has the right (one would say, the
moral right) to coerce its members into moral, 'ergo' human, existence, by making them live up to its moral standards, whether specific
individuals desire it or not.   In 'Odysseus und die Schweine, oder
das Unbenhangen an der Kultur', Lion Feuchtwanger mused on the
frightening possibility that Odysseus' sailors, once transformed into
pigs by treacherous Circe, liked what they experienced and refused to
be returned to the human shape.   For all Durkheim's discourse can
articulate, it might quite easily have been so, without in the least
undermining the 'necessity' of society or putting in question its
moral legitimacy.   Religion, far from being a bastard of human prejudice and a gaoler of the human mind, supplies the best pattern of
this unquestionable moral legitimacy being exercized properly, with
humane means matching humane ends.   Whenever 'intervention of the
group', which results in imposing 'uniformly upon particular wills
and intelligences' 'a 'type' of thought and action' takes on a form
of religious ritual, 'there is no question of  exercizing a physical
constraint upon blind and, incidentally, imaginary forces, but rather
of reaching individual consciousnesses, of giving them a direction
and of disciplining them.'   (17)   In an ideally functioning, technically wholesome society, men would, in Irving Hallowell's words,
'want to act as they have to act and at the same time find gratifi-
cation in acting according to the requirements of the culture' (18) -
or, as Erich Fromm put it, social necessities would be transmitted
into character traits.   (19)
By a curious distortion of perspective, it has become universally
accepted in the folkloristic versions of Durkheim, that his major
methodological postulate was that ideas are things and should be
explored accordingly.   Phrased in such a form, culled literally, but
out of context, from Durkheim's writings, this postulate looks simply
like another positivist profession of faith - an appeal to study
social affairs in the same way as natural scientists investigate the
natural.   This is not, however, the meaning bestowed on the notorious statement by the logic of Durkheim's theoretical preoccupation.
Before Durkheim asked the question of how things human were to be
explored, he had first inquired into the nature of things human.

The original inspiration, the springboard of the whole Durkheimian theoretical system, had been obtained from the problem set aside by Comte as, allegedly, self-evident and presenting no difficulty: what is this something, which is not present in non-human nature, yet confronts human beings with the overwhelming power typical of natural things?   What is this something, which is experienced with the thoroughness and resilience of things, yet bears none of the features we use to predicate of 'ordinary things'?   The answer – the really important one – was : ideas.   It is ideas which confront us as if they were things.   This allegedly revolutionary postulate, that ideas should be treated as things in the course of the scientific investigation, followed with a virtually tautological automaticity:  of course, things ought to be studied as things;  since it has been revealed that one sub-class of things consists of societally supported ideas, it is a matter of the simplest syllogism to draw the conclusion:  ideas ought to be studied as things.   Durkheim did not bother with trying to prove the major premiss (this has been awarded an axiomatic status by commonsense), nor the conclusion (this did not require any proof, following, as it were, from its premisses on the strength of logical rules).   His attention was instead focussed on the minor premiss:  some things are ideas;  this he, indeed, worked hard to prove.   The distinctive feature of Durkheimian sociology – one which has been taken over and absorbed by most of twentieth century sociology – was the decoding of the experience of the 'second nature' as a set of commonly held ideas, which impose themselves with invincible force thanks to the fact that they define the meaning of being human, moral, and good.

   This central idea of Durkheimian sociology has been subsequently presented (in what is perhaps a modernized, but surely an obfuscating version) as the view that what integrates society into a system confronting the individual as an autonomous, and superior, force, is universal allegiance to the so-called 'central cluster of values' – a dehydrated, hygienic brand of 'conscience collective'.   If pared to its bare essence and purified of essence-obscuring jargon, the idea becomes strikingly simple (simultaneously revealing its otherwise concealed self-limitation):  society, being the only setting for the human existence of 'homo sapiens', is therefore its members' conformity to the central, society-anchored ideals.   Therefore, if society does not perish, it is because of members' conformity to these ideals.   And this is good and desirable.   (Let us notice, in the anticipation of further discussion, two of the self-imposed limitations of this reasoning:  First, the existence of society serves anthropological needs, needs of men as members of the human species; hence, by definition, it is extra-historical and extra-partisan. Second, the justified need of 'a' society has been tacitly identified with the need of 'the' society, society which happens to define at the moment the meaning of being human.   This specific society is, of course, a historical phenomenon.   But having related it to an anthropological, extra-historical need, this theoretical perspective presents the historical as the natural.   Not so much by an explicit statement to this effect, but by denying the possibility of defining the meaning of 'being human' in terms not supplied and not legitimized by the society currently in existence).

   The history of much post-Durkheimian sociology has boiled down to an immanent critique of this simple, perhaps simplistic answer to the question about the nature of society's coercive power.   Durkheim's successors could not be satisfied for long with the generality of Durkheim's answer, as Durkheim himself could not quite swallow the generality of Comte's;  hence they attempted to dissect, cut and divide the 'central cluster' into its constituent parts, unexplored by Durkheim, and to reveal the morphology of the central ideals' ascendancy over human individuals.   This critique was immanent, since never once has the central pillar of Durkheimian sociology been questioned:  that what is 'thing-like' in the experience dubbed 'society' are ideas, and that, consequently, society remaining itself is above all an affair which takes place in the space stretching between minds.   Nor was the question of the price of 'being human' in the form so defined ever asked.

To give only the most original and sophisticated examples of the immanent critique, let us consider those modifications of the central theme which were introduced by Shils, Parsons, and Goffman.

In Shils's work, the role of central ideals (values) in sustaining and upholding the social whole is not denied;  but it is postulated that for their constraining impact on individuals' behaviour to be effective, other factors ought to mediate, to which Durkheim paid little or no attention.   It is therefore suggested that the mental grip of society over individuals has in fact a two-tier structure, aptly expressed in the concept of centre and periphery.   The central belief system of a society - so Shils tells us - is a high-level abstraction which can be apprehended only by way of a rather intellectually demanding philosophical analysis.   But ordinary people are not philosophers;  hence they come into the immediate presence of central values only on relatively few ceremonial occasions.   As long as these events last, the massive emotional attachment to central values is brought to a high pitch, loyalty is refreshed, hardened and reinforced, but not necessarily translated into mundane precepts relevant to the daily routine and able therefore to safeguard everyday conformity.   It is personal ties, primordial bonds (like kinship or quasi-kinship loyalties), partial responsibilities held in diverse corporate bodies - rather than ceremonially evoked beliefs - which secure the upholding of central values by the routine, institutionalized activity of the multitude of men.   So it is, in fact, the dense fabric of close relationships (face-to-face or formalized and role-related), and immediate tasks at hand, which channel human routine behaviour into conformity with central values, while the values themselves remain, from the perspective of ordinary men, inconspicuous, unobtrusive, even invisible.   And so the image of social integration, which Durkheim proposed to stretch over the whole of society, is compressed by Shils to the central nucleus of the social system.   It is this central sphere alone which consciously and articulately sustains and is sustained by the crucial ideals of society.   The peripheral sphere is not riveted to the central hub by ideological loyalty, but tacked to it by numerous strings of personal and not-so-personal bonds.

The strings which keep society together on various tiers are therefore different;  but all are spun of the same yarn of ideas. Shils points out the insufficiency of the 'central ideals' concept as an explanation of the persistence of 'social reality'.   But other concepts, which he introduces to support and to complement Durkheimian legacy, are made of the same raw material, and the 'some things are ideas' postulate remains in full force.   Only splinters of central ideals must be absorbed by all for society to survive;   but they have to be buttressed by a plethora of other ideals, like kinship or organizational loyalty (all of which are, of course, ideas which act like things), to serve their function.

The picture of a multi-tier structure of the value-based superiority of society (which Shils came across in his war-time study of German POW, and made public in 'BJS' in 1957) has been drawn in more detail by Talcott Parsons - in his theory of the levels of organization of social structure.   (20)   As we know, the entire Parsonian theory of society is organized around the concept of binding normative patterns, whose compelling influence on individual behaviour is achieved and continually sustained by the twin effort of 'pattern maintenance and tension-management' (preventive and penal action against deviation as well as positive inducement of conforming conduct), and 'integration' (mostly processes commonly described under the heading of socialization).   Normative patterns, as in Durkheim, reflect requirements of the social whole;   they specify those aspects of individual behaviour which are relevant to the common good and which must be observed if society is to survive.   Only if it succeeds in subordinating individual actions to such normative patterns, does society create a viable environment in which social action is possible.   Normative patterns specify, one could say, the most general and necessary conditions of social existence.

In his theory of the hierarchical organization of the social structure Parsons spells out the essential difference between his notion of normative patterns and Durkheimian 'ideals' embodied in 'l'âme collective'.   Normative patterns do not refer necessarily directly to the collective, societal aims, to the necessity of sustaining togetherness, communal co-operation, etc.   Through their own hierarchical structure they ultimately point precisely in this direction;   but, particularly in their lower, more specific and particularistic ramifications, they may well conceal this final target, visible only when seen from the top - in the scores of pernickety instructions apparently unconcerned with the welfare of the totality.

> The most general values of the highest level are articulated at successively lower levels so that norms governing specific actions at the lowest level may be spelled out... At the lower levels, norms and values apply only to special categories of units of the social structure, unless they are the norms most general to all 'good citizens' and therefore are couched mainly in terms of a personality reference.

In this way the most general and crucial norms, bearing directly on the survival of the society, are translated into secular, mundane briefings.   The majestic structure of the social system may be sustained without an explicit appeal to sacred sanctions.   It is buttressed by the routine, habitualized observance of commonplace usages rather than by the universal internalization of, and loyalty to, the loftier and more abstract articulations of the central value cluster.   In effect, the individual may well be unaware of the more remote, system-related consequences of his daily conduct.   From his limited vantage point, only a branch or two and a dozen twigs are

visible, while the rest of the tree may escape his notice without
impairing the smooth running of his everyday routine.  It is left
to the social analyst to reproduce theoretically the fine tissue of
dovetailing normative patterns, to make explicit their implicit
function, to show how indispensable they are for social action and,
indeed, the social existence of human beings.  We recognize the
traditional role of the priest - the interpreter of the intrinsic,
though concealed, wisdom of the Creation, the preacher of the good
which consists in the surrender and the joy which can be derived
from enthusiastically embraced necessity.  The scholastic principle
'ens et bonum convertuntur' supplies adhesive for the weaker joints
of the theory:  one cannot envisage existence without society, hence
it is good that society survives;  it can survive only if consensus
is secured;  this consensus is laboriously pieced together from
apparently petty trivialities;  let us, therefore, learn to see
through them, let us learn to perceive higher reasons in lowly rou-
tines, vital functions in vexing nibblings, the noble in the menial.
The overall effect of Parsonian 'hierarchization of consensus' - his
linking of the narrowest precepts to the survival of society, his
firm supposition that any specific demand coming from 'outside' the
actor's ends and motives, however difficult and incredible it may
seem, can be shown in principle to derive from the most crucial
commands of society's survival - amounts to a wholesale hallowing
and ennobling in a truly Leibnizian manner, of everything experienced in social life as real, including its most unsightly aspects.

The common assumption of both Durkheim and Parsons is that if a
meaningful (human, in the case of Durkheim;  effective, in the case
of Parsons) action of an individual is to be possible at all, the
same normative patterns or ideals must motivate and constrain the
behaviour of all the individuals partaking of the action.  What is
necessary, is - in the words of W.I. Thomas, to whom Parsons repeatedly acknowledged his intellectual debit - 'a group-organization
embodied in a socially systematized scheme of behaviour imposed as
rules upon individuals' ('The Polish Peasant in Europe and America').
Orderly, planned, organized, effective - indeed, free - human action
hinges on the successful enforcing of institutionalized patterns,
(even if they materialize, 'surface on the phenomenal level',
through the psyche of individual actors, they still constitute an
external reality, a 'second nature' from the actors' point of view)
being, as they are, imperative and, within the limits of the intended
action, unavoidable.  It is this indomitable 'second nature' which
safeguards the complementarity of expectations - this paramount condition of human action.

There is double contingency inherent in interaction.  On
the one hand, ego's gratifications are contingent on ego's
selection among available alternatives.  But in turn,
alter's reaction will be contingent on ego's selection and
will result from a complementary selection on alter's part.
Because of this double contingency, communication, which is
the precondition of cultural patterns, could not exist
without both generalization from the particularity of the
specific situations (which are never identical for ego and
alter) and stability of meaning which can be only assured
by 'conventions' observed by both parties.  (21)

Throughout his work, Parsons appeals to the pan-human fear of uncertainty, unpredictability, of the bizarre, the extra-ordinary and
the surprising.   Such fear, very much an anthropological phenomenon
(in the sense of being associated inexorably with all and any human
action), is double-pronged:  the terror of 'things' going wild and
responding to routine and skilful handling in an unusual, unforesee-
able way, and the horror of 'persons' confounding all expectations by
using an unreadable symbolic code or attaching inscrutable meanings
to known signs.   It is this fear which the smoothly and coherently
articulated society promises to dispel.   It offers freedom from fear
in exchange for conformity to 'conventions'.
     One of these conventions, and a paramount one at that, is the
division of roles and their differential treatment.   Role-require-
ments are on the whole clear-cut.   They spell out the expected re-
sponses to ordinary stimuli.   When known to both protagonists of an
interaction, they will provide the sought-after 'stability of meaning'
during the exchange.   The partners enter their interaction 'pre-
fabricated', processed by society, with the meanings of their acts
firmly attached to their possible actions well in advance, as the
appurtenances of the assumed role.   Meanings are not negotiable,
they are given from the start or some time before the start, and the
only outcome of a departure will be a distortion of communication.
But then all the frightening spectres of a disorderly, unpredictable
world will promptly return.   They are kept at a safe distance only
inasmuch as everybody holds on to the role he has been allotted;  and
unqualified acceptance of one's share in the essentially unequal
allocation of rewards society is able to offer is the 'conditio sine
qua non' of an orderly world.
     Such attractiveness as the Parsonian version of Durkheim's idiom
possessed can be ascribed to the irresistibly facile solution it
offers to the haunting feeling of uncertainty emitted by the opacity
of human condition.   Docility is the only price one is asked to pay
for one's security;  and the goods (only if everybody else respects
his debts) will be surely delivered on payment.   At the same time,
the costs of insolvency have been raised to nebulous heights;   the
choice is now between order and chaos, security and pandemonium,
quiet haven and uncharted turbulent waters.   When faced with such a
choice, it is easier to remain docile and to accept one's share,
however inferior and unjust it may seem:  there is, it seems, no
alternative.   The Parsonian model of 'social nature' suppresses the
alternative, which is the most important distinctive function of all
conservative, dominant ideologies.   By presenting this suppression
as, in its essence, a matter of values people respect and obey, he
adds cogency to ideological attractions:  the idea is attuned to the
established formula of wisdom and legitimacy.
     Coercion is necessary - this is the central message of Parsonian
theory.   It has, to be sure, a reassuring quality, as any science-
backed statement reaffirming intuitive hunches of commonsense will
inevitably have.   The Durkheim-Parsons line in sociology is an elaboration of the leading themes of commonsensical experience and,
within the horizons of this experience, the only intelligible elaboration.   When the life situation of men is constituted by market
exchange, considered to be the only mechanism through which conditions of individual survival may be furnished, the individual can-

not but keep trying to reorganize his social environment in tune with
his interests and ensuing desires;  but so will everybody else.   The
resulting world would be at best technically untenable, at worse a
hell painted by a surrealist, if it were not for some form of coercion or another.   One can say that this market-type of freedom requires coercion as its necessary supplement;  without it, it would
never furnish conditions sufficient for the survival of the society
or, indeed, of the individual.   Parsons's message is not, therefore,
a lie.   On the contrary, it sums up what seems to be a fair and
conscientious description of the society as it is and as we know it.
In so far as we live and wish to remain alive in a society organized
as 'an opportunity-structure for the fulfilment of an egoistic individualism'  (22)  we view as a nightmare (and call it 'jungle law')
the absence of coercive power strong enough to curb the very egoistic
individualism we crave to fulfil.   If there is a contradiction
between these desires, it is by no means caused by the frailties of
human reason and cannot be corrected by improving on human logic:
it is, in fact, a reflection of the genuine incompatibility between
equally powerful commands of the existential situation - a situation
from which there is neither a good nor unambiguous way out.   And so
coercion is unavoidable.   The only choice available within the
horizon drawn by the institutionalized market, is that between 'hard'
and 'soft' coercion;  at least since the time of Kant, we have been
keen scrupulously to distinguish between compulsion coming 'from
without' and that coming 'from within', and to evaluate them differently.   We prefer internalized coercion to that which is brutally
external, reaching for physical force where indoctrination failed.
In this sense, Parsons has given us the description of the good
society:  a description which we may consider realistic because it
does not transcend the horizon of the present, but which depicts
society as it might be, rather than the one which is.   The Durkheim-
Parsons society is founded entirely on 'soft' coercion;  it is a
successful society, which thanks to the triumph of its moral power
can well-nigh renounce its physical force.   This society may be seen
as the utopian projection of the liberal market principle.   For this
reason - while eliminating alternatives to this principle from the
range of options considered as feasible and worthy of informed argument - it may play a critical role, acting toward pushing the 'humanization' of an essentially inhuman predicament to its accessible
limits.   It is, therefore, a 'reformatory within conservative'
attitude, embedded and codified in a vision of social reality which
posits coercion as inevitable, but coercion's more unsightly forms as
superfluous.   Its utopian edge may be brought into relief when
people face the uglier alternative struggling for actualization;
hence the celebration of 'Durksonianism' inspired by the discovery of
Nazi and Stalinist horrors;  and the embracing of 'Durksonianism' by
the mildly critical, mildly conservative 'middle-stream' intellectual
movement in the Communist East.

One version of the Durkheimian idiom, however, draws the immanent
critique of 'conscience collective' to its limits by bringing to
light the oppressiveness contained in the 'soft' form of coercion
itself.   It was Goffman alone who openly attacked and rejected outright the 'schoolboy model' which undergirds the image of society as
mostly a teaching-learning institution with a modest sprinkling of

correctional measures – the model which Goffman ridicules by its very description:

> If a person wishes to sustain a particular image of himself and trust his feelings to it, he must work hard for the credits that will buy this self-enhancement for him; should he try to obtain ends by improper means, by cheating or theft, he will be punished, disqualified from the race, or at least made to start all over again from the beginning .

One can easily distinguish behind this description the noble view of society as a mainly humanizing, moral force, which both Durkheim's poetry and Parsons's prose have keenly promoted. In Durksonianism, mutual trust based on integrity and truthfulness is the 'limen' towards which society strives and which all its institutions try to work hard to bring about. If something is being suppressed on the way, it is the animal instincts and a-social egoism of individuals who are treacherous and untrustworthy until they have undergone redeeming social treatment. Without society, men are crude, cruel and dishonest; thanks to the coercive power of 'conscience collective' (or central values cluster) they are turned into moral beings.

Not so, says Erving Goffman. Fresh from the bedlam of McCarthyism, Goffman hastened to articulate the staggering discovery of the generation: just how wild society may run when overwhelmed by the zeal of its moralizing mission. This discovery furnished Goffman with his main, and perhaps only, motif, on which he has harped obsessively in all his work. The new experience was there, ready to be wrapped in words. But Goffman, in tune with the long established habit of sociologizing without history, did more than just that: he promoted the intuitive findings of a generation into another general model of society. What had been done by human beings tinkering with their history, was polished up as another face of the 'second nature'.

And so we learn from Goffman, that such freedom as the human individual may possess is obtained not thanks to society, but in spite of its obtrusive invigilation. The central issue in the individual-society relation is not, as Durksonianism would have us believe, the joyful and rewarding, though society-controlled, immersion of the person in the refreshing, purifying, humanizing waters of socially-upheld ideals and recipes. Instead, it is the precarious and hazardous art of surrendering, or pretending to surrender, to as tiny a modicum of social 'musts' as is humanly possible, in order to be allowed to enjoy one's virtual, and always lonely, existence. Socialization, once again in sharp opposition to Durksonianism, is the price paid in exchange for a makeshift emancipation from unbearable social surveillance, rather than the royal highway leading to the full, truly human existence. Society and the individual, far from imitating the benevolent teacher and his diligent pupil, bear a striking resemblance to mutually suspicious, shrewd and malevolent hagglers. They would not, though, go as far as annihilating the other partner or foreclosing his property; they need him as much as they seek to cheat him and to get the better of him. Intertwined forever in their equivocal hate-love, they will be only too happy to settle for keeping the other side at a safe distance, and will be eager to accept the other side's promise to behave as 'it befits it to behave' as the conditions of armistice.

If the person is willing to be subject to informal social

control - if he is willing to find out from hints and
glances and tactful cues what his place is, and keep it -
then there will be no objection to his furnishing this place
at his discretion, with all the comfort, elegance, and no-
bility that his wit can muster for him ... Social life is an
uncluttered, orderly thing because the person voluntarily
stays away from the places and topics and times where he is
not wanted and where he might be disparaged for going.  (23)

And so society is still the 'tough reality' which confronts the
individual with the stubbornness and impermeability of things, but
it is a reality of a pile of conventions and excuses, false pretences
and 'white lies', rather than majestic ethical principles.  Society
emerges under Goffman's pen as a gigantic hoax, patched up by a multitude of puny deceptions and confidence games.  It is a pseudo-
moral system into which scores of individuals are tacked together
with the strings of sham devotion and make-believe acts.  Everybody
there pretends to do something he neither does nor wishes to do.
Society is, therefore, put back again in the dock from which Durksonianism strove hard to extricate it.  It is again reduced to pure
constraint, to negativity eo ipso, to a set of border-stones rather
than guide-posts, aimed at imposing willingness to desist action
rather than willingness to act.  The rule of society is sustained by
the massive conformity of individuals - no departure here from the
axiom of Durksonianism.  But what makes society tick is, in Goffman's view, the multitude of human beings, simply keeping obediently
to where they have been declared to belong, donning eagerly the mask
offered by society, and once in a while emitting the right noises
which indicate that they love the mask and would not swap it for anything else.  'Perhaps the main principle of the ritual order is not
justice but face.'  Indeed, little has been left of the lyrical
romance of the beast ennobled or the epic of the affectionate monster
made rational.  What is left of social reality, what the individual
must still scrupulously learn and observe, what the individual is
still forbidden to defy, what is presented to the individual as an
uninfringible, hard and 'objective' reality - is a particular set of
rules which regulate the bargain for face and for the frontiers of
the private domain.  These rules refer to interhuman communication,
to the way in which it is made meaningful and effective, but not to
the content of the message.  Not beliefs, but rules of the game glue
together the Goffmanesque social order.

What is being exchanged in human encounters, which combine into a
process called 'society', are impressions rather than goods.  The
partners give each other clues which help the 'alter' to locate his
protagonist on the cognitive map.  The locating, so it seems, is the
important thing, rather than other, more tangible benefits, which can
be derived from the interaction.  One can assume (though Goffman
never gives it away in so many words) that what men are after is
above all cognitive certainty and the emotional security which comes
with it.  Hell is the Other, one would say with Sartre;  the very
presence of the Other makes my own 'whatness' problematic, questions
the comforting obviousness, 'givenness' of my existence, and compromises me, gives away things which I would rather keep for myself.
The feeling of constant vigilance by the Other, of my being watched,
spied upon, assessed, is a source of constant fear.  Society helps

us out:  it opens a huge store room of protective masks, disguises,
make-believe attires behind which we can hide, thus making our own
'whatness' opaque, impervious to an undesirable eye.  From the open
expanse of truth and authenticity we flee under the secure circus
tent, where everybody pretends to be somebody else, everybody is
aware that the others are not what they seem to be, but nobody cares
any longer about what they 'really' are.  Having once donned the
clownish mask, people are determined to squeeze as much pleasure as
they possibly can from the mimicry.  If we have to play the game,
let us make it grand.

And so what the individual offers in interaction are expressions.
Of the two kinds of expression - 'the expression that he 'gives' and
the expression that he 'gives off'' - the second, which 'involves a
wide range of action that others can treat as symptomatic of the
actor, the expectation being that the action was performed for reasons other than the information conveyed in this way' (24) came to
play in Goffman's writings an increasingly central role - as it does,
in his view, in social life as such.  It is not enough to be X and
to behave the way in which people expect X to behave;  one has, in
addition, to convince others that he indeed behaves like an X, that
he 'is' X.  The second need comes to overshadow the first;  it seems
that in fact it eliminates the first or, at least, gains independence
of it.  The view that the second has been built on the sound foundation of the first (conveying and disseminating such a view is the
very intention behind the second category of expressions) reflects,
again, sham pretences rather than a necessary connection.  In fact,
excelling in the first expression is not a sufficient condition of
overall success;  what is more, it is not even the necessary condition of such success.  Display is a separate art in social encounters and perhaps the only art which keeps the delicate social
fabric in balance.  As a result, what is called 'social reality'
appears to the individual to be not just unmanageable, but impenetrable as well.  Certainly he tries to pierce through the masks which
cover the faces of his partners in the life drama - but pretences
have been piled upon pretences and, like the gripping discovery of
Ibsen's Peer Gynt, there is no 'hard core' in the onion, just layer
behind layer, however conscientiously you try to penetrate the
'ultimate depth'.  Goffman's imagery is meant to explain not just
why we experience 'society' as a reality, but why this reality is
opaque and, in the end, impervious to our eye.  We are left with the
impression that society must remain so to survive.  The play of pretences is the essence of all and any social relations.  The effort
to dispel the mist will result, at best, in an endless chain of app-
roximations, hardly ever conclusive.

For Durkheim, in order to be human, the individual has to embrace
the morality which society propounds and supports.  For Goffman, in
order to be himself, the individual has to defend himself against
society by using socially produced tools of disguise.  The 'second
nature' image has thus come full circle.  It had started, at the
beginning of modern times, as a man-legislated tissue of power relations which may have, in principle, violated 'laws of nature'.
Through a truly dialectical 'negation of negation' it emerged, with
Goffman, as a 'must' everybody takes part in generating and keeping
alive, but hardly deliberately, and without ever surveying the whole

structure.  It is now the human individual who sets the standards of
human nature.  'In interiore homine habitat veritas'.  Society is
again experienced as too tight a collar.  If anything, it tends to
obfuscate and confound human truth.  It stands between the individual
and his truth.  It breeds immorality and it feeds on immorality.
Society is now perceived as pure negativity.  It is something the
individual has to fight all his life.  He may, as in fact he does,
adjust himself to these conditions of perpetual struggle, but the
outcome of adjustment is hardly Durksonian 'humanization'.  Society
is degraded;  once the natural and logically indispensable locus of
human life, it has been reduced to an inhospitable and demanding environment.

The about-face in the perception of the 'second nature', exemplified by Goffman, may be alternatively portrayed as a further 'peeling
of the onion' of social reality.  The experience of constraint had
been ascribed at the beginning to faulty political institutions.
The discovery of which sociology as 'science of society' was begotten
consisted in unravelling another, deeper and tougher, reality beneath
the realm of politics;  this was mostly conceived as made of ideational stuff, but somehow sedimented and toughened to the point of confronting any individual or group of individuals with the force of
genuine 'things'.  The intensive analysis of the texture of these
sediments, as well as of the process of sedimentation, has led in the
end beyond the layer of social institutions, towards the individuals
themselves, who are the ultimate source of all and any social institutions and 'social reality'.  It is the attempt to peel further the
onion of social reality which has been proclaimed somewhat pretent-
iously as the current crisis of sociology.


'SECOND NATURE' AND THE COMMONSENSE

Sociology, as we know it, was born of the investigation of the regular, the invariable, the unmanageable in the human condition.  In
its most zealous and pietistical moments it tends to conceive its
own activity in terms of the crusade of science against 'the mystical
notion of free-will'. (25)  In more sober and secular moods it
readily grants the individual his idiosyncrasies, but declares them
scientifically uninteresting:  the field of sociological investigation begins where the unique, the unrepeatable and irreplaceable ends.
It does not deny human freedom;  it simply evicts it beyond the
boundaries of scientific inquiry.  The latter makes sense only when
concerned with the unfreedom of uniformity.

Sociology, as we know it, inquires into the 'conditions' of the
normal, but the 'causes' of the abnormal.  'The normal' is, in its
pre-predicative, intentional meaning, whatever is recurrent, repeatable, expected to happen again and again within the territory delineated by the interested human eye.  The abnormal is, eo
ipso, whatever should not happen under given conditions, but did.

Nothing is bizarre in itself.  The oddity of a phenomenon is
never an attribute of its own - though this is what the common figure
of speech would have us believe.  We perceive an event or an object
as odd when it 'stands out' from the colourless, jejune background of
monotony.  But the background in turn is the product of selective

perception;  it is the act of sowing standard seed which turns other
flowers into weeds.   It makes little sense, therefore, to blame
sociologists for ignoring or belittling the role of individual (by
definition irregular) factors.   This 'negligence' is as 'organic' to
the activity of sociology as its constitutive interest in the nature
of social reality;  one, in a sense, follows from the other.

The notorious difficulty experienced by bona fide sociologists
whenever they attempt to account for the subjective, the spontaneous,
the unique (in their own terms rather than in terms of their margin-
ality or obsolescence, from the perspective of a supra-subjective
whole) - is an immanent feature of sociology, unlikely ever to be overcome from within this intellectual project.   All systematized knowledge of human life process, sociology included, is an attempt to
lend intelligibility and cohesion to unorganized, disparate commonsensical experience;  it is a sophisticated elaboration upon crude
commonsense, theoretical refinement of the raw material of the 'directly given'.   This knowledge may be sceptical and critical of the
naive beliefs of commonsense - an attitude in which established sociology takes well-deserved pride.   But commonsensical experience
will always remain the locus in which sociological queries and concepts are gestated - and the umbilical cord binding the knowledge of
human affairs to commonsense will never be cut.   The commonsense is
the ultimate object of sociological exploration in the same inescapable way as nature is the ultimate object of natural science.   Even
its care-free trust in the 'objective reality' of the social, sociology owes to the commonsensically confirmed pre-predicative experience of unfreedom.   It is this experience which provides the
ultimate, and the only, foundation for social reality, and therefore,
for sociology as a legitimate intellectual activity with a legitimate
and 'objective' subject-matter.

The trouble with commonsensical evidence is, however, that it is
equivocal.   It does not contain information about the external determination of human fate and conduct.   On the contrary, such evidence it acknowledges of nature-like, stubborn resistance to human
will, can only appear as the corollary of a manifestation of this
will.   The experience of freedom is possible only as a sense of sub-
duing an outer force, perceived, because of its resistance, as 'real'.
Similarly, the sense of unfreedom, styled as perception of reality,
manifests itself only in the form of defeat of a project impelled by
human will.   The aspects of experience which can be articulated,
respectively, as freedom and unfreedom, appear either in conjunction
or not at all.   Knowledge of unfreedom (constraints, nature, reality
- all these family of concepts, meaningless unless traceable to the
same pre-predicative source) without intuition of freedom is as
absurd and, indeed, inconceivable, as experience of freedom unaccomp-
anied by knowledge of its potential or actual limitations.

Hence any system of knowledge (including sociology), which describes the structure of unfreedom alone, is a one-sided account of
human experience, and needs additional constructs to foreclose its
unaccounted-for components.

It remains to be shown, this time in disagreement with commonsense,
that what appears to the pristine, pre-predicative experience as a
free act, stemming from reasoning and choice, is an inevitability concealed and invisible to the naked eye.   Much of the disdain shown

towards commonsense, written into the project of science, has as its
source the alleged inability of unrefined experience to discover the
necessary and the law-like behind the façade of free will.   This
ineptness of unaided commonsense to uncover the sternly deterministic
tic order of the world and to account for its own hidden causes also
provides the stuff of which the distinction between 'essence' and
'existence' have been ultimately forged.   The impression usually
given, and often deliberately enhanced, of scientific knowledge being
an implacable enemy of commonsense (while, in fact, remaining its
symbiotic adjunct) is due mostly to this circumstance.   Science is
expected only to 'explain' how the necessity of the outer world -
already experienced as nature-like - comes into being;  but it has
to 'prove', in defiance of pre-scientific experience, that the kingdom of necessity embraces the totality of human life processes.   The
second task, naturally, takes much more effort and consequently generates much more zeal.   It is, therefore, the second line of the
battle where the heaviest artillery of science is concentrated and
the most ferocious barrages are launched.   The war is waged between
the 'real order of things' and misleading appearances - the 'mystical
notion of free-will'.

Both tasks, to be sure, stem from the poignant need constantly
generated by the lived-through human experience.   Men experience
resistance coming from a misty realm which is not like those impenetrable, tough, tangible things they freely conceive as objects.   As
one might expect, they keep asking how it can be that that 'something', divested of all the familiar attributes of material objects,
nevertheless behaves like them in setting limits to human movement.
The intuitive metaphor requires intelligible substantiation, and the
riddle sets loose all the imaginative power of theorizing and model-
building.   This is the cognitive curiosity aroused by the unknown
and the incomprehensible.   The concepts produced in response are
meant to bring sense, order, to unintelligible experience.   The
message conveyed by this experience is clear;  its structure is not,
however.

But the other task is supported no less eagerly by the life process.   The experience of free will is by no means an enjoyable
feeling.   More often than not it is psychologically unbearable in a
world posited as a set of chances which may be taken up but can be
missed.   In such a world, free will is experienced as an 'agonizing
burden', (26) as 'dizziness', which 'occurs when freedom looks down
into its own possibility'.   (27) A man cannot easily tolerate the
knowledge that his predicament is of his own choosing, his failure of
his own making.   Freedom means choice, and the choice is - if it is
real and concerned with genuine crossroads and the options which
count - one agony men dread more than any else.   There is an air of
irrevocability to each act of choice:  for each road chosen, there
are many abandoned once and for all.   Choice is, therefore, the
gateway through which finality enters the open-ended and hopeful
human existence;  choice is the point at which the unnegotiable past
gets hold of the amenable future.   The experience of freedom is,
therefore, an inexhaustible source of fear.   If the experience of
nature arouses curiosity and creative energy ('only in the name of
something not of my own creation can I usurp the want of creation')
(28) this other experience generates an overwhelming urge to escape.

It is not knowledge, paving the way for free action, which is sought, but, on the contrary, a powerful authority contradicting the evidence of experience, exposing its frailty and undependability.   What is wanted above everything else is the removal of the burden of responsibility.   Free will in itself is an unfathomable well of anxiety. Free will, conceived as the only cause of constraint, irrevocability and finality in human fate, is a nightmare.

God is thereby generated at both poles of the human experience. On the 'reality pole', as He who set the world clock.   On the 'free-will pole', as He who pre-determined human fate and conduct, while refusing human creatures the ability to discern the inevitable behind the phantom of their free decisions.   On the first pole, He stands as just a name for the obviously known;   He adds little to the content of human experience.   On the second pole, however, He is an alien, powerful force, suppressing and re-moulding the data of experience.   It is here that He is particularly desired and most intensely awed.   Here His presence does not contain its own proof and requires all the emotion and power of belief for it to take root. Naively and intuitively, men know their responsibility, but dread the knowledge and wish to suppress it.   If they experience their relation to the world as antagonism, they feel much more comfortable if the play in which they act is staged and directed by an imperious, high-handed director.   Perhaps it is not the frustration itself, but the awareness of one's own fault which induces most of the suffering, and is most difficult to withstand.

Religion has always built its spiritual power on this essential need which stems from men's confrontation with their world.   The priests in all their many garbs, whether those of Radin's 'religious formulators', or Eliade's 'shamans', have always acted as the mediators between the Director and the actor whom He moves over the stage without divulging His intentions or the denouement of the plot. Each actor knew only his own few lines, and could surmise only that his part dovetailed somehow, somewhere, into the parts of the other members of the cast and combined with them into a meaningful whole. No conclusive proof that it did indeed do so could he derive from the lines he knew.   Deep in his heart a terrifying suspicion gnawed at his very ability to take part in the show: life was but a walking shadow;   it was a tale told by an idiot, full of sound and fury, signifying nothing ... But to admit this to himself, to articulate this intolerable dread, was to refuse to act, to reject life and to choose death.   It was the job of the priests to see to it that the suspicion never surfaced;   in this they co-operated with the man-made structure of the life-process, designed in such a way as never to give the opportunity for ultimate questions and final choices. The priests had to mount a convincing case for the existence of the Director.   And then they had to interpret His design, never unveiled by the Author himself in the presence of the uninitiated. They had to demonstrate the meaning behind the absurd, the plan behind the random string of unconnected events, the supreme logic peeping through the endless chain of personal defeats.   The belief that one is nothing but a pawn in the superior player's hands removes unhappiness from bad luck.   It is a benign, charitable belief.

Its antagonist is the doctrine of free will.   It is the idea of free will, continuously suggested by daily experience, which has to

be suppressed in the first place for God to relieve men of the tormenting realization of their immense task.   God's therapeutic job
of reconciling men to their fate cannot be completed so long as the
slightest remnants of the free will doctrine linger in human consciousness.   Pelagianism was, therefore, the most treacherous and
subversive of all heresies with which religion had to wrestle.   It
was Pelagius' view that God's grace is a reward for human merit rather than its condition.   The view could easily ruin the subtle therapeutic design of the church: were it accepted, men would have to
struggle for God's grace and to blame themselves were it not forth-
coming - to wit, to go through all the agonies which they sought to
escape when embracing their belief in God.   It was, therefore,
against Pelagius that St Augustine loosed his most poisonous arrows.
In doing so, he formulated the original theory of deviation, later to
be taken over and re-phrased by Durksonianism: God's grace precedes
all merit and is the preliminary, necessary condition of human
virtue.   The latter is inconceivable without the active intervention
of God.   If man breaks loose, if he defies God's command, if he
attempts to stand on his own feet - sin is the only possible result.
No merit awaits man on his road to independence.   The distance he
adopts in relation to God is the measure of his deviance.   Amidst
the crumbling and decomposing souvenirs of the most grandiose civilization mankind had known to date, with the terrors of the great
Barbarian Unknown just across the gate, Augustine evoked God as the
last retreat of steady ground amidst the earthquake: 'With a hidden
goad thou didst urge me, that I might be restless until such time as
the sight of my mind might discern thee for certain'. (29)  The god
is in the embracing of God.   Since his fall, man's free will, if
unaided by God, can lead only to morbid sin.   It is only God's grace
which fills the empty container of will with the desire to do good.
One can say, in anticipation of the future vagaries of Augustinian
anti-Pelagianism: it is the powerful force 'over there' which makes
man a moral being.   To escape the perversions lying in wait in the
wilderness of the will considering itself to be free, man has to 'put
himself in Him who made him', adjust himself to his predicament, embrace it willingly and gratefully.

   The Durksonian deified society will later inherit such redeeming
potentials of God.   The Durksonian vision will take over Augustinian contempt for the sinful, beastly flesh and the location of the
morally ennobling reunion with God in the higher regions of the
Spirit - the 'situs' of belief, trust, and self-constraint.   Durksonian sociology will take over the traditional function of the
priest:  the interpretation of the supra-individual order, modelling
the inscrutable into intelligibility, imposing an iron-clad logic
upon seemingly irrational, chance events, lending meaning to apparently nonsensical human fate.   Contrary to Nietzsche, God is not
quite dead.   Demystification of the human community has taken on
the form of deification of the communal sources of individual unfreedom.   The perpetual effort to satisfy cognitive and emotional
needs fomented by daily experience has not stopped.   It is not
likely that it ever will.

   Whatever the veracity of sociological models and the reliability
of their verification, they owe much of their credibility to the
degree of intelligibility they lend to the protean human experience,

and to the extent to which they match the criteria of acceptability as fixed by experience-determined urges.   In other words, the more chance a sociological model stands of being absorbed by common-sensical wisdom and, with time, of being perceived as obvious, the stronger the case it makes for the inevitability which resides in the human life-setting and the more relief it offers to the 'dizziness of freedom'.   The mainstream sociological conceptualizations of pre-predicative experience were always distinguished by their demonst-rating the determinism of human action and revealing the hidden sense of phenomena whose wisdom and utility was not immediately apparent.

This was, indeed, the ubiquitous tendency in the prevailing brand of sociology, as exemplified by Durksonianism.   Such Wrong-style complaints as were levied against the allegedly 'oversocialized' con-cept of man proclaimed by this sociology were misdirected, since the concept of socialization was not an empirical description of human behaviour, but an analytical postulate commensurate with God's grace and aimed at the same task of rendering human fate intelligible and bearable;   far from being an error to be easily corrected to the be-nefit of the ruling paradigm, it has been its 'sine qua non' attri-bute and paramount source of strength.   No other secular form seems to be available for promoting the idea of the essentially determined character of human conduct.   If society replaced God in the role of the source of necessity, socialization is a natural substitute for the God-operated springs of human deeds.

Socialization is, indeed, a well-nigh wholesome substitute.   It meets at one fell swoop cognitive and emotional pleas pressed by both poles of human experience:   it binds one pole to the other, creating a situation in which the explanatory formulae attached to either con-firm and reinforce each other.   To the cognitive query:   'what is nature-like in the human setting?', the answer is:   'the socially-supported moral ideas which confront you with the stubborn reality of things'.   To the emotional anxiety arising from the experience of freedom and choice an answer is given which is derivative of and complementary to the first:   free will is an illusion, in so far as whatever you do, has been impelled by the ideas you have absorbed from your social environment;   the selfsame moral (cultural, norm-ative) ideas which society has been inculcating in you from your birth on.   It is society, therefore, which simultaneously makes you what you are and bears the responsibility for it.   Sociology fought the 'illusion of free will' with the doggedness and zeal which the religious doctrine of providence previously manifested.   The fact that religion fought free will as heresy, whereas sociology has fought it as a 'mystical', i.e. unscientific, notion - cannot con-ceal the striking affinity of attitudes and intellectual projects.

In fundamentalist sociology, as in fundamentalist religion, the major, 'noble' determinism in human conduct has had, however, all along, a competitor:   a different kind of determinism, usually ass-essed as somewhat inferior, less worthy, better to be got rid of, though never entirely eliminable.   This feature of a dual determin-ism or the dual sources of inevitability in human behaviour perhaps owes its persistence again to commonsensical experience, whose evi-dence it articulates.   It is, however, a different aspect of the experience it reflects.   This time it is not the essential split of experience into nature—like constraints and the intuition of free choice, but the perception of acts as differentially valued, as divided into commendable and condemnable, allowed and prohibited by a superior power - sometimes felt as situated 'within', sometimes as coming from outside the acting individual. All system is a limitation, an exclusion of some occurrences on behalf of some others - and social systems, which delineate the outer framework of human life are no exception to this rule; hence the manichaic streak in intuitive experience is fairly universal, positing at all times a troublesome problem for fundamentalist world views. To be complete and cohesive, such a world view had to account for the fact that despite the presence of superior and, in essence, benevolent (good, humanizing) power (God, society), acts which cannot be tolerated and ought to be assessed as negative (sin, deviance) do occur on a more or less permanent basis. Answers to this challenge occupied the whole continuum from the outrightly manichaic solution to that which tried hard to steer clear of manichaic temptations, and which, in the end, put in question the omnipotence of the central power. As we know, the official doctrine of the Christian Church took a sharply antimanichaic stand. It was accepted, again from the time of St Augustine, that evil is a purely negative phenomenon rather than another 'substance': evil is the non-possession of grace and derives from the inability of the wan, imperfect human creature to reach the 'ought' prescribed for him in God's mind; the possibility that God may be somewhat less than omnipotent, or - worse still - that He might be a source of evil as well as the source of good, was considered unacceptable. Not so in sociology. Its solutions were, on the whole, akin to the Christian tradition, in that it never permitted anyone to doubt that deviant acts occur in spite of the dominant tendency of society rather than as a result of it. In all other respects, however, the sociological tradition was much more tolerant to manichaic ideas. On one hand, the occurrence of deviant, and by definition disruptive, acts was traced back to the technical imperfection of the many means applied by society to keep its members in check - to the society which was not quite up to the task. On the other, particularly in the Adam Smith—Max Weber tradition, departures from the 'normal' pattern sponsored by society were ascribed to the intrinsic, or residual irrationality of human action - and, in particular, to the emotional, non-intellectual layers of human personality. The essential incompatibility of the affectual and the rational, of emotion and reason has been an unquestionable truth to virtually all sociologists; superiority of the second over the first has in fact been taken for granted, though the terms in which it has been articulated varied. By Comte as well as by Weber, this superiority was organized along historical lines - the rational system superseding that founded upon affection - and was thereby projected as the axis of societal progress. Sociologists, on the whole, side with the social practice which tends to denigrate, condemn and suppress drives defined as 'biological', deriving from the human animal infrastructure and in opposition to those socially inspired and legitimized. They, therefore, posit their own formula of objectivity and truth-pursuit as the historical tendency of the human world as such. This theme is found beyond the enthusiastic welcome given by Comte to the coming industrial age, this positive age which should be 'matched' only by a similarly positive science of human affairs.   One can find the same theme, though presented in a considerably refined manner, in Weber's diagnosis of the trend towards the legal-rational society.   It is this society, in which men are increasingly prompted to act according to the rules of instrumental rationality, which lends ultimate sanction to the plausibility of an objective social science:  ideal types, positing the behaviour of a rational actor in given circumstances, will approximate more closely to actual conduct in conditions where other bases of social action, and, above all, traditional and affectual, recede to the margins of social life.   The final triumph of objective knowledge over the emotional, the subjective, the pre-social, parallels the historical tendency towards the institutionalization of rational objectifications of socially selected behavioural patterns.   The sociologists' neglect of the non-rational aspects of human experience is increasingly justified by the consistent elimination of such aspects, or their diminishing social importance, as a result of social development itself.

The above reasoning squares well with another tendency of sociology - that is, to seek the meaning which occurrences derive from their relation to the societal whole, rather than from intentions of actors.   Kingsley Davis was in a sense right in declaring a separate 'functional method' to be a myth, and proclaiming the concept of function to be constitutive of sociology as a whole.   It is true that thinking in terms of 'function' has been consistently much more widespread than any particular school which identified itself with such usage.   Having assumed once and for all that it is society which defines the conditions of human life, which shapes human 'nature', sociologists could, without further argument, depict as the meaning of a recurrent or single social event, its role in sustaining and perpetuating this very activity of society.   It is the calculus of function, therefore, rather than ordinary logical calculus, which decides the meaningfulness of customs and rites, institutions and usages.   It is no longer the individual reason of 'les philosophes', but the impersonal, invisible reason of society, which decides whether a social phenomenon does, or does not, make sense. What seems to be absurd and despicable to individual reason, may still be utterly 'logical' from the wider and more objective vantage point of society, from which its function becomes evident.   If the reason of 'les philosophes' was Protestant in spirit - each individual reads the Bible, each has the right to interpret its meaning - sociologists took the line pursued by the Catholic strategy of communication with God mediated by professional priests, who are alone in their ability and their right to uncover the hidden meaning and sense in the allegedly inscrutable verdicts of God.

The great achievement of a sociology which developed as the science of unfreedom has been the unity of its ontology, methodology, and cognitive function.   The grip in which sociology has successfully kept human imagination is strengthened by the fact that it is 'based on these objectifications of reality which we undertake daily', that it 'merely extends the everyday procedure of objectifying reality', as Habermas pertinently observed.  (30)  It is fed by the pre-predicative experience of the life-process as essentially unfree, and of freedom as a fear-generating state, and it aptly supplies apposite

cognitive and emotional outlets to both intuitions.  It merely reinforces the intuition of unfreedom, and the supremacy of the outer
condition over individual cravings.  It makes this unfreedom less
intolerable by positing its inherent wisdom and coherence.  It
assists the individual in his spontaneous effort of disposing of the
excessive, and, therefore, anxiety-ridden, freedom of choice, by
either positing this freedom as illusion or advising him that such
freedom is supported by reason which has been delimited and defined
beforehand by society, whose power of judgement he cannot challenge;
not only because of its superior strength, but simply because the
distinction between reason and unreason is synonymous with the division between society and non-social, i.e., animal life.

Sociology, therefore, as the science of unfreedom, answers the
call coming from the perplexed individual searching his own experience for such meaning as can make it acceptable.  It placates that
experience which is vexed and confused by the incompatibility of
individual freedom with the actuality of the life-process not of the
individual's choice.  It saves the individual from the torments of
indecision and the responsibility he is too weak to bear, by sharply
cutting down the range of acceptable options to the size of his
'real' potential.  The price it pays, however, for playing such a
benign and charitable role is its essentially conservative impact
upon the society it helps people to explain and understand.

It has become increasingly popular, mostly in politically motivated quarters, to accuse established sociology of a vulgar 'distortion
of truth', of uniting with the powerful in praise of their order and
in their effort to convince the oppressed and the duped of its intrinsic virtue.  The critics who wish to expose the genuine role of
sociology in the struggle of groups and their ideas, tend to look, it
seems, in the wrong direction.  They seem to identify the partisan,
ideological function with propaganda in favour of the superior qualities of a specific type of social system;  hence they assume that
their case will be proved if they can show that sociologists, while
pretending to be impartial and objective, in fact smuggle into their
allegedly non-partisan descriptions attitudes heavily laden with
partisan values.  Hence analysis of the cultural role of sociology
often takes the form of a peculiar 'value-hunting'.  The game the
hunters are after is proof that sociology is 'bourgeois ideology',
and this proof will take the form of a demonstration that, explicitly,
or implicitly, sociology extols the virtues of a bourgeois society
and inspires, or tries to inspire, popular sympathy for its attributes.

The hunters are on a false track.  A strong case has been repeatedly made on behalf of 'value-freedom' which sociology has achieved,
or strives towards with a measure of success.  Sociologists do
agree with Comte, when he protested against 'metaphysical thinking',
which exaggerated 'ridiculously the influence of the individual mind
upon the course of human affairs', and called for man's nature to be
given 'a solemn character of authority which must always be respected
by rational legislation' - in short, to 'assume the ground of observed realities'. (31)  In so far as this observable reality
towers high above the level of meagre individual capacities, the
truth of sociologists towers high above the truncated, partial truths
of individuals or groups of individuals.  Sociology contains no

more partisan values than the reality it describes has incorporated
and petrified.   But sociologists do take one fateful decision:   to
remain entirely on the ground of this reality, not to transcend it,
to recognize as valid and worthy knowledge only such information as
can be checked against this reality here and now.   The alternatives
which this reality renders unrealistic, unlikely, fantastic, sociology promptly declares utopian and of no interest to science.   In
this, and perhaps in this alone, resides the intrinsically conservative role of sociology as the science of unfreedom.   Sociology acts
on the assumption that social reality is regular and subject to recurrent, monotonous uniformities;   by making such an assumption, it
posits social reality as conforming as much as possible to that description.   By positing it in such a form, sociologists perpetuate
belief in the 'natural' rather than the historical character of
social arrangements.   In other words, it is not true that sociologists take conservative attitudes in order to lend support to, and
extol, bourgeois virtues;   they may inadvertently lend such support
if reality they 'naturalize' happens to institutionalize such
virtues;   but then it would offer similar service were other principles the object of institutionalization.
    The stance of 'techne' (in opposition to gambling, random  acts,
etc.) may be applied only to objects which are essentially constant
in their behaviour, and therefore predictable.   Hence positing the
social world as nature, subject to a repeatable cyclicality described as laws, is a necessity for any knowledge which intends to serve
the technical interests of men.   And sociology, as we know it, does
desire to serve such interests.   If human institutions are to be
treated as objects of technologically informed manipulation, they
must be seen as law-abiding units of nature-like reality.   At any
rate, they are of interest to sociology only inasmuch as they fit
that model.   As Bernard Berelson once candidly put it, 'The ultimate
end is to understand, explain, and predict human behaviour in the
same sense in which scientists understand, explain, and predict the
behaviour of physical forces or biological entities or, closer home,
the behaviour of goods and prices in the economic market'.   (32)   It
is only natural that such an end be seen and portrayed as impartial
and free of earthly commitments apart from the universal human
desire to know in order to act.   Within the limits of a given
society any knowledge which such an end may beget is, in a sense,
impartial.   There is nothing, indeed, in the knowledge itself
(though a lot in the surrounding social conditions) which pre-deter-
mines its exclusive utilization by one rather than another part of
society.   The intrinsic bias of such knowledge lies elsewhere - in
its stubborn (though prudent, considering its aims) refusal to transcend the horizon fixed by the prerequisites of the technical interest
alone.   But this can hardly be held against knowledge which frankly
concedes its commitment to the technical-instrumental service.   To
be at peace with itself, to remain faithful to its pledge and deliver
the goods it has promised, sociology has to resist resolutely the
temptation to reach beyond the boundaries of reality here and now -
the only object of a technically sound and effective action.
George Lundberg, that most outspoken interpreter of the programme of
positive sociology, could indeed be righteously indignant when faced
with demands (or accusations) that sociology ought to be (or is) a

politically committed endeavour:

> I am opposed to making science the tail of any political
> kite whatsoever ... I have emphasized that political scient-
> ists are indispensable to any political regime.   Social
> scientists had better work toward a corresponding status ...
> The social sciences of the future will not pretend to dictate
> to men the ends of existence or the goals of striving.   They
> will merely chart the possible alternatives, the consequences
> of each and the most efficient technique of arriving at what-
> ever ends man shall from time to time consider it worth while
> to pursue ... No regime can get along without it.   (33)

To be fair, a 'Wertfrei' sociology would shirk from the vexing issue
of the social responsibility of scientists no more than natural
scientists have done, 'wertfrei' as they are to everybody's satisfaction.   But the contention is that the fact that human beings are
objects which sociology helps to manipulate, does not posit the issue
of responsibility and commitment in a qualitatively different light.

Indeed, Lundberg's point is almost trivially true.   No ideological gulfs between regimes seem to bear much relevance (freak historical variations notwithstanding) to their uniformly keen interest -
sometimes unrecognized, but always 'objectively' present - in the
kind of technical service so cogently exposed in Lundberg's programme.   There is little doubt that this programme is really 'neutral'
in terms of ideological divisions, that is to say, in terms of those
specific models of social organization the virtual or would-be mana-
gers of social processes would wish people to love or, at any rate,
to enact and to perpetuate through their orderly behaviour.   Such
partisan commitment as may be sensibly imputed to this programme is
of an entirely different nature and cuts across existing (as well as
possible, conceivable) political camps.

Logically, social science may influence human behaviour - perform
the 'engineering' function - in two different ways.   If 'engineering'
consists, by definition, in the shaping or re-shaping of an object by
factors external to it and designed without its participation, then
the distinction between the two is determined by the very structure
of human action, as it has been schematically portrayed:

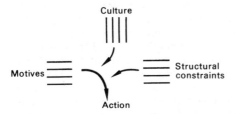

Granted that the individual's motives remain (unless processed culturally) beyond the reach of the factors dealt with by social science
proper (these motives may be acted directly upon by drugs, brain
surgery, etc.), there still remain two openings through which an outside influence may penetrate the course of the action and modify it.
The first is, broadly speaking, the 'cultural' opening.   It conveys
those cognitive assertions and normative precepts which the individual employs to assess the situation he confronts and to select the
'right' (that is, commendable in one of its many senses, e.g.,

effective or morally elevated) course of action.    The individual's
motives processed by such cultural factors and applied in order to
assess the relative value of different courses of action is in fact
the meaning of the widely used concept of the 'definition of situation'.    The factors which enter the action through the cultural
opening are aimed precisely at the definition of the situation.    By
supplying the actor with new information about the environment,
about himself, and about their reciprocal relations, with knowledge
of new ways of acting, or with the image of possible ends of action,
these factors may prompt the actor to change his view of the situation and its eventual consequences, or, on the contrary, to strengthen his attachment to the previous definition.    For example, by
exposing intimate links between the limits of individual gratific-
ation and freedom of action on the one hand, and societal networks
of power and wealth (normally invisible to the unaided individual
eye), the private experience of individual suffering and frustration
may be transplanted from a 'consumer deprivation' intellectual scheme
into a 'class exploitation' scheme.    Accordingly, subsequent action
may be re-directed from the industrial, trade-oriented context into
the total, society-inscribed one.    Or, by connecting the diverse
components of individual strivings and accomplishments into a communal unit styled as the nation, the tendency to consider the nation
as the prime object of loyalty, together with the ensuing propensity
to ethnocentric behaviour, may be reinforced.

The 'cultural' factors appeal, therefore, to individual consciousness.    They tend to broaden individual vision, to indicate new, unsuspected horizons from which to review and to assess the individual
'raw' experience.    To be accepted, and therefore effectively to re-
shape the conduct of the individual, they must match, in a sense, the
individual demand:    they must be perceived as being adequate to the
personal experience so far accumulated and sedimented in the individual's private and group memory.    This acceptance (or, for that
matter, rejection) is subject to the rules of logic (though not necessarily to the truth of the message, rules of logic formal as they
are).    They are likely to be appropriated if they 'make sense', i.e.
if they render meaningful and intelligible the available knowledge
of the individual situation, and lend apparent coherence to the disparate odds and ends of the individual's previous experience.    The
probability of their acceptance will be further augmented if, in
addition, they succeed in pointing out a hopefully reliable way of
resolving a task experienced as unpleasant, or stabilizing a situation felt as satisfactory.    Their rejection, on the other hand,
will by no means be inevitable, unless they appear grossly to con-
tradict previously amassed, experience-supported knowledge.    Cultural factors, to conclude, can direct and re-direct human action
by offering new vistas (supplying new factual knowledge), or 'arou-
sing the conscience' (supplying new values).    In both cases, they
widen the range of choices cognitively and morally accessible to the
individual.    Consequently, they extend the freedom of the individual's action.

Now, any given volume of individual and/or group experience
allows for more than one meaningful interpretation.    'Adequacy' is,
first, a matter of degree;    second, it can hardly ever be ascert-
ained conclusively unless put to the practical test.    There can,

therefore, be more than one intellectual scheme, which renders the experience intelligible and thus makes a strong bid for acceptance. And acceptance or rejection is, on the whole, a matter of competition and practical trial.  In the process, these aspects of the interaction between experience, cultural formulae and action are revealed which have been, in various ways, subsumed under the name of ideology. However the term 'ideology' is defined, it refers to a phenomenon whose essence is neither a distorted relation between a message and the 'reality' it purports to portray, nor a partisan, unscientific attitude supposedly impelling some action on the part of the author. The attribution of the term 'idological' refers in fact to the specific way in which the ideas in question – those affecting individual definitions of the situation – are adopted or rejected as interpretations of reality and guides to action.  Their apparent partisanship and endemic inability to live up to the exacting stipulations of 'consensus omnii' result not so much from their intrinsic flaws and formal defects, but from the persistent diversity of the individual and group predicament and experience, which ultimately wields the key to social praxis.

The simultaneous presence of several competing cultural formulae, coupled with the impossibility of assessing in advance their adequacy in terms of multifarious individual and group experiences – to determine their possible application – results in 'cultural engineering' acquiring the form of a continuous discourse, in which verbal exchanges alternate with practical tests.  The assimilation of cultural formula requires the active stance of the person or group whose definition of the situation is to be reformed.  In the process of enlightenment the initiative is perhaps distributed unequally, but as the process develops the distinction between subjects and objects of action tends to be blurred.  The cultural influence prompts the activity of the actor, both theoretically and practically; it puts the actor in a situation of active choice and forces him to re-analyse his own conduct and its relation to the social setting in which it takes place.  New and alternative cultural formulae enable the actor to take a detached posture toward his own activity, to approach it as an object which can be objectively scrutinized and reliably evaluated.  Putting the actor on the outside of his own life routine, it may liberate him from the shackles of habit, irremovable as long as they are unreflected upon.  In short, influencing human action through the process of enlightenment, through cultural discourse, is an agent of freedom.

Unlike the cultural constituent of human action, the 'objective' structure of the actor's situation, usually presented as 'structural constraints', has little to say concerning the ends and meanings of individual or group praxis;  its only role in the general scheme of action consists in setting the ultimate limits to the actor's 'sensibility' – in classifying possible actions into the realistic and the abortive.  It will decide which courses of action, of those the individual or the group may take, stand a chance of success, and which are, from the start, out of the question.  In other words, structural constraints delineate the boundaries of individual or group freedom.  The field of freedom may be vast or narrow, depending on the degree to which the situation is structured.  Theoretically, it is possible to narrow it enough to make the pursuit of a specific end as improbable as is required in a specific case;

either because a rational individual would balk at an admittedly unrealistic effort, or because such an effort, even if, for the lack of
relevant information or understanding, he were to make it, would lead
him nowhere.   This remarkable quality of structural constraints can
be, in principle, exploited by anybody who would like an individual
or a group to take or to abandon a specific course of action.   This
time, however, influence will be exerted directly on the structure
of the situation rather than on its definition (i.e., on the external
setting in which action takes place, rather than on the consciousness of the actors).   The effectiveness of such influence will not
depend on willingness to accept the end as true or morally justified;
it certainly does not include a discourse, and eliminates the possibility of role-exchange between participants of the process.   On
the contrary, it assumes the permanent inequality of status and the
split between the subject and the object of influence.   Hence the
knowledge the influencing agent employs is effective or ineffective
regardless of the experience of the human objects whose conduct it is
about to shape.   This experience is, therefore, irrelevant and can
be disregarded in the process of verification (or falsification) of
the knowledge in question;   and - in so far as such conditions hold -
those human objects may indeed be looked upon as 'things', no different from the objects manipulated with the help of the natural sciences.   In this sense, Lundberg's insistence on the non-ideological
character of the knowledge he proposes to pursue is well justified.
The technical-instrumental handling of human objects is indeed a
foundation on which a bona fide empirical-analytical science of
human affairs can be safely erected.

The practical application of science advocated by Lundberg may be
described as an engineering-through-situation, as distinct from the
previously discussed engineering-through-definition-of-situation.
To exemplify the Lundbergian type of engineering, let us consider a
typical situation reduced to the simplest diadic form.   In this case,
the scheme of influence will assume the following shape:

  i  A is confronted with alternative action X or Y;
 ii  B wishes A to take the action X;
iii  B may then use available assets either to increase rewards
attached to X or to maximize the punishments attached to Y.
 iv  Following iii, A is now more likely than before to take the
action X.

If all these events happen, we can say that B has indeed 'engineered' the action of A, with the important qualification, however,
that in the situation of the type described above, what is being
'engineered' is the probability of a specific action, rather than
the action itself.   However immense B's assets, he will never
achieve complete mastery over A's conduct in the sense of excluding
all possible alternatives.   A's definition of the situation is an
irremovable link in the chain of events leading to the final decision.   Still, one can approach very closely indeed a predicament
practically indistinguishable from 'inevitability', if B succeeds in
lifting the price of alternatives high enough.   B does it by man-
ipulating directly the structural constraints which delimit the freedom of A's choice and action.

A, therefore, has been an indirect object of B's action, A's
situation being this action's direct object.   The knowledge B has

required to set A in the kind of motion he wished is information of
the statistical probability of a specific action being increased or
decreased depending on the re-arranging of the elements of the
actor's situation.    If the images and definitions supplied by sociology of a Durksonian type – one aimed above all at satisfying the
need of intelligibility – can exercise its technical-instrumental
role only through the consciousness of actors, the kind of knowledge
serving the second type of engineering has been developed in the so-
called 'behavioural sciences'.    To obtain such knowledge, one has
to arrange, in B.F. Skinner's words, a 'repeatable bit of behaviour'
in a 'causal chain consisting of three links: 1 an operation performed upon the organism from without – for example, water deprivation;
2 an inner condition – for example, physiological or psychic thirst
and 3 a kind of behaviour – for example, drinking'.    The second
link is, however, 'useless in the control of behaviour unless we can
manipulate it'.   (34)  We can therefore disregard this link, as we
do the 'mysterious notion of free will', as the element which will
contribute nothing to our results.    Analytically, it is argued,
human behaviour posits no problems essentially different from those
encountered, say, in the exploration of flies' conduct;  and as for
the latter, 'if no one calculated the orbit of a fly, it is only
because no one has been sufficiently interested in doing so'.    Well,
there is still one difference:  all knowledge, if available to all,
can in the case of humans (though not in the case of flies) turn into
a self-destroying prophecy.    To this objection Skinner resolutely
retorts:   'There may have been practical reasons why the results of
the poll in question could not be withheld until after the election,
but this would not be the case in a purely scientific endeavour'.
(35)  The type of technical-instrumental interests behavioural sciences aspire to serve have no use for the consciousness of controlled
actors.    If it appears in related arguments, it is only in the role
of an irritant which would be better disposed of entirely.

The knowledge sought in the above case, therefore, when effectively applied, can be kept away from the individuals or groups whose
behaviour it is about to influence.    Far from being a mere technical
expedient, this is an integral trait of the knowledge in question.
It cannot but polarize men into those who think and act, and those
who are acted upon, into subjects and objects of action.    It is not
true that such knowledge disregards all consciousness, values, ends
– that is, everything 'subjective'.    It is only the motivations,
preferences, norms and beliefs of the objects of control-through-
reinforcement which such knowledge evicts into the field of the irrelevant.    Naturally, there is no intention to communicate with them
or, indeed, reform;  no question of knowledge as a dialogue may even
be posited within the universe of discourse defined by the programme of the behavioural sciences.    In this sense, the output of
behavioural sciences is indeed ideologically neutral in the same way
as bureaucracy,   whose vantage point it employs to perceive the
world as manipulable without committing itself to any specific end
of manipulation – and thereby positing the manipulation as a technical problem.

But is the technical tool of behavioural knowledge available to
all who may wish to employ it for the advancement of the ends they
cherish?  Skinner, to be sure, is aware of the problem:  'It is true

that we can gain control over behaviour only in so far as we can control the factors responsible for it.   What a scientific study does is to enable us to make optimal use of the control we possess'. 'Us' obviously means here, people who are already in control of the resources necessary for the application of behavioural findings. The type of knowledge which behavioural sciences are intent on supplying does not interfere with the extant distribution of assets;   if anything, it will have a 'funnelling' effect, emphasizing and further polarizing present inequalities.   'Us', therefore, rather than universalizing human status in relation to the benefits science can offer, divides men sharper still into two highly unequal groups. The marvels of 'neutral technology' will probably be of greater use to a prison governor than to a prisoner, to a military commander than to a private, to a general manager than to a clerk, to a party leader than to a rank-and-file member.   The kind of engineering which is catered for by behavioural sciences is therefore committed and partisan from the start (though not in the usual ideological way), in the sense that it reinforces the already existing split between subjects and objects of action, the controllers and the controlled, the superiors and the subordinated - and renders its elimination even more difficult than otherwise would have been the case.

One should not lightly dismiss, however, the enlightenment impact still exercised, though inadvertently, by behavioural sciences. The image of men and the mechanism of their action propagated by these sciences may induce the tendency to perceive the world as a set of manipulable objects, and the life process as a set of technical problems rather than questions which, to be solved, require communication and discourse.   The yearning for wisdom and meaning will then degenerate into a demand for technical instruction of the 'do it yourself' sort, and the problem of meaningful life will be reforged into the question how to 'win friends and influence people' and to otherwise outwit one's brethren.

Of the two brands of sociology, which acts programmatically as the science of unfreedom, one brand, therefore, tends to reinforce the harsh realities to which the second tends to induce men to reconcile themselves.   Each, in its own way, plays in culture an essentially conservative role.   Each tends to suppress, in its own way, alternative forms of social existence and to identify the historically created situation, either conceptually or in practice, with nature-like reality.

However well such sociology may serve the perpetuation of everyday life, informing the mundane daily routine (in its engineering-through-definition role) and enhancing the efficiency of the network of power (in its engineering-through-situation role), its inability to account for the persistent experience of human freedom and to assist its promotion engenders time and again dissent and rebellion.

# Chapter 2

# CRITIQUE OF SOCIOLOGY

## THE HUSSERLIAN REVOLUTION

As we have seen, it is commonsensical, mundane experience which lends plausibility to the sociological explanation of human existence. It is thanks to this powerful and ubiquitous support that sociology may neglect the task of testing and proving the legitimacy of its own activity. Its legitimacy is taken for granted, assumed as being borne out by the flow of everyday experience: it is only the way of keeping it so - that is, the technical problem of accuracy and precision in fulfilling the task whose validity is beyond question - which remains problematic.

And so sociologists rarely look into the foundations of the sumptuous edifice they erect and adorn only from the ground floor up. Indeed, the attitude taken by sociology to its own ultimate source is strikingly reminiscent of that peculiar blend of embarrassed reticence and neurotically ostentatious disdain with which a 'nouveau riche' of humble origin often treats his ancestry. Officially, sociology is the critique of commonsense. In reality, this critique never goes as far as fundamentals and never brings to light the shared assumptions which render both commonsense and sociology meaningful. It is perhaps precisely because of this close and intimate kinship that sociology can never set itself outside commonsense at a great enough distance for these tacit premisses to become visible. Pragmatically, such a long stride outside the secure field would be patently unwise. To question the reliability of the ontological evidence supplied by commonsense would certainly mean an earthquake, which could easily shatter the whole edifice of the science of unfreedom. Even a naive, philosophically unrefined reflection on the validity of commonsensical experience reveals how much emotional security and self-righteousness rests on how brittle a foundation. As Robert Heilbroner put it: (1)

> to the ordinary person, reared in the tradition of Western empiricism, physical objects usually seem to exist 'by themselves' out there in time and space, appearing as disparate clusters of sense data. So, too, social objects appear to most of us as things ... All these categories of reality often present themselves to our

consciousness as existing by themselves, with defined boundaries
that set them off from other aspects of the social universe.
However abstract, they tend to be conceived as distinctly as if
they were objects to be picked up and turned over in one's hand.
As in the quoted paragraph, even the very beginning of the scrutiny
reveals two things which sociology normally is reluctant to discuss.
First, our ontological knowledge of the 'objectivity' of categories
of reality is ultimately based on the fact that they appear to the
ordinary person as such;  and this appearance is never naive and
pure, but a result of a complex process of training.   Second, the
allegedly unshakeable obviousness of objectivity is, in fact, constantly produced and re-produced by an intrinsically tautological
process.   The ontological premisses of empiricism derive their
proof from commonsensical perceptions which deliver such proof only
because they themselves have been trained for the purpose by the
assumptions they are supposed to validate.

It is from this circular process of sham validation that Husserl,
and phenomenology, purported to liberate our knowledge.   They saw
the way to this emancipation in the critique of tolerated, rather
than consciously accepted, commonsensical assumptions.   Having conceived of the process of knowledge as a self-enclosed, hermetically
sealed field which is set in motion (and, consequently, capable of
being reformed) all by itself, Husserl identified the task of re-
storing human knowledge to a sound and unshakable foundation with that
of purifying the nuclear experience from foreign, inadmissible admixtures.   The first element to be separated and purged was precisely
the tacit assumption of existence, on which belief in the validity of
the sociological exercise (as well as of many other similar exercises) was buttressed.

Husserl's project was a resurrection of an old preoccupation of
philosophers rather than the positing of a question previously un-
asked.   Its staggering impact was due to the fact that Husserl re-
stated, publicly and forcefully, ideas not daily present in an age
in which empiricism was too well established to bother with vindicating the truthfulness of its claims.   Potentially, however, they
had remained an integral part of the Western philosophical tradition
long before Husserl recovered them from the remote corner of the intellectual storage room, to bring them back into the focus of philosophical analysis.   Indeed, such ideas were current as far back as
the beginnings of the Western philosophical tradition in the works
of Plato and Aristotle.   It was Plato who questioned, more than two
thousand years before Husserl, the solidity of that knowledge which
may be derived from the 'mere' existence of a phenomenon;  real
truth resides in extemporal ideas and can be sought by insight, by
unmediated intimation with the necessary.   By the same token he
ascribed to the existence of objects a somewhat inferior, and above
all unstable, protean, accidental status: it followed that genuine
knowledge could not possibly rest on such a shaky, moving foundation.
As for Aristotle, he carefully separated essence from existence, as
a category in its own right, and - most important of all - autonomous in relation to existence.   The information 'that' something is,
throws little light on the question 'what' is it.   Existence is
accidental to essence and, therefore, does not illuminate it;  on
the other hand, existence is not included, and therefore cannot be

derived from, the essence of things.   This latter motif, in particular, was later broadly discussed by Avicenna, and it was through his works that it was brought to the attention of, and keenly absorbed by, modern European philosophy.   With the advent of a science wed to technical-instrumental interests, it was instrumental in the gradual abandonment of 'essences' as the barren ground on which no useful information with technical import could flourish.

The essence-existence dilemma has always sprung to the attention of philosophers in the epistemological context.   Its importance was derived from the centrality of the question 'how do we know what we think we know?', or, more specifically, 'how can we be sure of the truth of our knowledge?'   The great achievement of modern science consists precisely in the fact that it has managed to make its everyday activities, and the utility of their results, independent of any answer which one could give to these questions, thereby evicting the questions themselves beyond the boundaries of its own self-sustained system.   Not unless a science faces an ontological crisis do such questions become again an integral link in its validating logic. Since, however, these questions have no points of communication with the ordinary daily practices of science, it is highly unlikely that they will ever be imposed upon scientists by the logic of their own inquiry.   If at all, they will come from the regions normally considered as external to science - again an occurrence which is highly unlikely in view of the institutionalized autonomy of the scientific community.   The so-called social sciences, to be sure, form an exception to this rule:   because of their wide lay audience and their decision to select commonsensically accessible experience as their subject, they can never succeed in subjecting their object to their exclusive rule, or in fortifying their autonomy by the ordinary means of professional elitism guarded by self-selection. Whatever the reason, the social sciences are the only ones which  are organically incapable of purging themselves of the epistemological question once and for all.   Unlike the natural sciences, their positive findings and their sheer meaningfulness hinge directly on the stance taken towards this central problem.   However hard they try, social sciences cannot separate epistemological issues from the object they choose to investigate.   That is to say, it is on these issues that the reliability of the 'obviously given' existence of social objects ultimately depends.

To this question St Augustine gave a virtually Platonic answer, later to be turned by Husserl into the cornerstone of his philosophy: 'You, who wish to know, know you that you are?   I know.   Whence know you?   I know not.... Know you that you think?   I know.   Therefore it is true that you think.   It is true'.   (2)  No certainty of existence is given to the human thought with such an obviousness as to render further questioning redundant - apart from the certainty of the thought itself.   The fact of thinking is the only indubitable reality which is given so clearly that it does not require any proof.   More than twelve centuries later Descartes will make the bold step St Augustine was prudent to eschew:   in the famous 'cogito ergo sum', he will suggest that the actual existence of the thinking subject, aside from the fact of thinking, is directly given in the unmediated experience:   therefore, the question of whether at least one object - the 'substratum' of my thinking - exists, is answered

conclusively by the very act of thinking.   In such a way the thinking subject validates simultaneously the essence and the existence.
One can draw reliable information concerning both from the same
source and by virtue of the same act.   This was, in fact, a daring
and fateful departure from the previous philosophical tradition
originated by the ancient sage.   What Descartes in fact suggested,
was that existence is as necessary and self-imposing as the truth of
the essence.   This might have played an important 'go-ahead' role in
times when the infant sciences had to look carefully over their
shoulder at their clerical watchdogs - but the patchiness of the
alleged reconciliation was something which could not be concealed for
long from the philosopher's eye.   After Descartes, just as before
him, philosophers continued to divide themselves into those who deni-
grated intellectual insights in favour of sensual impressions and
those who - faithful to Plato - could not but deplore the unrelia-
bility of 'creeping empiricism'.

Moses Hess was perhaps the first bluntly to declare as fake the
majestic logic of the 'cogito'.   He stressed that Descartes had no
right whatsoever, on the strength of obviousness alone, to jump from
the awareness of thinking to the assumption of 'substantia cogitans',
and from there to the reality of causal relations, allegedly warranted by the same immediacy.   Hess's metaphor was a child looking into
a mirror and believing that there must be another object behind his
impression;   the child eagerly peeps behind the mirror, only to find
to his bewilderment, a dark surface impervious to his eye.   The conclusion is terrifying:   either we succeed in substantiating our knowledge by the very act of thinking, or it will forever rest on moving
sands.   Husserl, in a way, picked up this task where Hess, having
had it barely sketched, abandoned it.

Husserl would settle for nothing less than establishing, beyond
doubt, the conditions on which we can obtain and possess knowledge
which is necessary, that is to say, independent of contingent existence, essential, in the sense of showing what things really are
instead of in what form they happen to appear, and objective in the
sense of being independent of any arbitrary meaning which a psycho-
logical, objectifiable, subject may wish to give it.   To achieve
such a purpose, Husserl proposed to end the millennia of separating
ontology and epistemology:   the two questions, which constituted two
philosophical disciplines, can be answered either together or not at
all.   'How do I know?' and 'what things are?' are, in fact, one
question unjustly and misleadingly split into two.   The only knowledge I may possess is precisely the knowledge of what things are.
Knowing is the knowledge of essence, of inseparable attributes of
things.   And knowing is the only way in which essences 'exist'.
'Being' is 'Bewusstsein' - being known;   'cogito' and 'cogitatum',
'noesis' and 'noema', are in fact concepts which try to catch the
same act of consciousness, though from different sides.   'Noema'
refer to the act of 'noesis' looked upon from the point of view of
its results;   but 'noesis' refers to the 'noema' seen as their mode
of being, of 'Bewusstsein'.   The only existence of things of which
we know for sure, clearly and without doubt, is precisely their
'givenness' as essence - the kind of knowledge-existence implacably
denied or neglected by empiricism which focussed on contingent appearances.   Meaning, essence, 'Bewusstsein' are created and maintained

together in the only act which is given directly, obviously, and without mediation: the act of intentional consciousness. The concepts of subject and object, which the dominant philosophy taught us to employ to describe our world and our way of being in it, are just abstractions which ossify arbitrarily isolated aspects of the virtual 'Bewusstsein'.

But necessary, essential, and objective truth is hidden from our insight by the 'natural attitude' - the careless, naive way of contemplating the world, in which objects appear to us as simply being present 'over there', independently of 'noesis'. The natural attitude is, to be sure, hardly 'natural'; it is a complex product of a multitude of uncontrolled assumptions and information which are taken for granted and never checked. One cannot embark on the thorny road to truth without first 'losing' this world which is ablaze with phoney appearances and misleading beliefs. The first thing to be left behind is all the information we possess or deem to possess of the 'existence' of things. Not that things do not exist 'over there'; but that their existence or non-existence is simply irrelevant to the pursuit of truth, and their objectified existence 'over there', in a mode different from 'Bewusstsein', can add nothing to their essence.

Hence the whole series of 'transcendental reductions', which must be performed in order to render pure 'noesis', untainted by external admixtures, accessible to our insight. The series starts by 'bracketing away', or 'suspending', the question of existence. We simply bar all considerations of existence of things from entering our reasoning. But there are other reductions as well, and one of them is the 'monadic reduction' - one aimed at purifying consciousness of all influences of culture, which shares with existence its contingent, inessential appearance. At the end of the long process of reduction a pure subjectivity emerges, thoroughly cleansed of all the misleading assumptions which refer to the allegedly 'matter of course' existence. One of the many assumptions which has been reduced away and left behind in the process, is the psychologists' notion of individual consciousness, considered as an 'object' over there, which can be objectively explored 'from outside' and duly described in an objectified language. Thus the sediment left at the bottom of the solution, from which all alien bodies have been scrupulously distilled, is not the individual psyche, but 'transcendental subjectivity' which has little in common with the Cartesian 'substantia cogitans'. It is set in motion by intentionality, instead of causality. It has been made, by the act of multiple reduction, impervious to causal bonds with the world, describable in terms of relations between objects.

There are several ways in which the critique of sociology can draw inspiration from the Husserlian philosophical revolution. All of them, to be sure, are related to the Husserlian re-evaluation of realities rather than to his specific findings and proposed solutions. First is the Husserlian restoration of subjectivity to the status of a valid - indeed, the only valid - subject-matter of knowledge. One can now invoke the authority of Husserl in objecting to behaviourist extremisms. Second and more important, is the peculiarly active meaning which Husserl, following Brentano, attached to his notion of subjectivity: it is an entity characterized above all

by its intentionality, the only active element capable of generating
meanings and, indeed, creating things themselves in their only reliable modality of 'Bewusstsein'.   These critics weary of the sociologists' irritating habit of objectifying meanings, of tracing them to
supra-individual entities like society or culture, and of focussing
attention on the means by which these meanings are brought from 'outside' to 'inside' the individual mind, may greet with relish a res-
pectable philosophy which offers its authority in support of the reversal of exploration.   Now one can start from the individual as
the pristine origin of his world, while enjoying the intellectually
comforting feeling that this decision brings emancipation from un-
welcome a priori assumptions, that is, genuine liberation from
commonsense - that perpetual criterion of the success of the avowed
scientific enterprise.   Third, the Husserlian treatment of meaning
supplies the sought-for means of lending radicality and cohesion to
the methodological principles of hermeneutics.   Not only is meaning
('Meinung') a derivative of intending ('meinen') rather than an
attribute of objects, but it provides all the reliable information
about things one can reasonably hope for.   Meaning is not something
which on principle can and ought to be compared with things 'as they
are', and which is, therefore, immanently crippled by that morbid
kind of subjectivity whose presence in scientific cogitations requires continual apology.   On the contrary, meaning is simultaneously the only source and the only sense of 'Bewusstsein' - the only
existence which can be legitimately and sensibly discussed by anybody wishing to grasp the true knowledge of things.   Fourth, one can
sense, in the emancipation of the validity ('Geltung') of meaning
from the actual process of thinking, the way out of the many methodological traps with which the traditional exploration of meanings
seemed to be inextricably associated.   According to Husserl it is
existence alone which depends on actual thinking, dealt with by
psychologists;   not the meaning  itself, situated in the transcendental subjectivity.   One can, therefore, validly explore meanings
without incurring the wrath of methodological purists who have justly
condemned introspective exercises for their heavy reliance of the
personal idiosyncrasies of the individual researcher.   Meaning is
not an entity uniquely located in the mind of an empirical individual,
but something transcendental to each individual consciousness and
therefore accessible to all.   The exploration of meaning may now be
pursued without mediation:   the empirical realm, subject to the
inter-subjective techniques of scientific observations, need not be
entered at any of its stages.   The vexing problems of intersubjective
verification, which arises immediately whenever (but only when) such
transgression takes place, can therefore be mercifully avoided.   By
the simple expedient of declaring the 'objective referent' irrelevant
to the question of validity of meaning one brushes aside the very
possibility of questioning the legitimacy of his explorations.   The
essential definitions of phenomenology surround its territory with a
dense line of turrets and moats which render its methodological fortress invulnerable.   One can indeed agree with Fink or Scheler, that
one cannot understand phenomenology without being a phenomenologist,
and that once having become a phenomenologist, one can view with equanimity inroads coming from outside:   they are doomed to peter out
the moment they break into the fortress.   Even the obvious objection,

that various phenomenologists, employing faithfully the same method of reduction, may arrive (as they actually do) to widely different intuitions of meaning, makes sense only within the activity organized by notions of 'objective truth' or 'being as it really is in itself': an activity to which Husserl explicitly denies anything approaching an ultimate authority, conceding it at best only a partial, derivative status. The diversity of intuitions signifies perhaps that the practice of reductions has been somewhat short of perfection - but it hardly undermines the validity of the method as such. As it were, Husserl never ascribed the meaning-giving activity to 'a' knowing subject; knowing subjects only attempt - sometimes unsuccessfully - to penetrate, to reflect upon, the meanings which are already 'given' by the transcendental subjectivity much in the same way as they used to be given by the scholastic God.

Practically, all these aspects of the Husserlian project may inspire a kind of research in which the techniques traditionally identified with empirical activity are relegated to a somewhat subordinated status. Instead of supplying outright the sought-for information about 'reality', they will be treated now as only a raw ore from which the actual metal is to be smelted. In the empirical activity, the chain of reasoning has been reversed. Husserl called for the application of multiple reduction to uncover the 'transcendental subjectivity' buried under numerous layers of objectifying abstractions. In the empirical research, which Husserl's appeal may generate, the hidden presence of transcendental subjectivity is taken for granted and the question is asked how, in actual fact, this presence makes human discourse possible. That this transcendental subjectivity (or whatever other name is used to denote it) is already there and operative, is not something to be demonstrated. It is taken as proven by Husserl, and therefore employed as a data-organizing, analytical device, even if it is not articulated and is, indeed, ineffable.

I have spoken thus far about the inspiration which one can derive from the Husserlian programme, rather than from Husserl's philosophy as a foundation upon which one could mount a system of sociological knowledge. The decision has been deliberate. Though there are few immanent limits to inspired, though free, interpretations, mounting a sociology upon Husserlian foundations does present difficult problems to which no one, to date, has offered an impeccable solution. Sociology, it is true, has been a family name for an odd gathering of images and activities which, sometimes, barely communicate with each other. Yet, even at loggerheads with each other, these images and activities have been recognizable as 'sociological', because of their common reference to the space extending 'between' human individuals. To be classified as sociological, an image or an activity has to relate itself to the phenomenon of human interaction. This self-defining act transcends the most vehement disagreements between schools, normally evolving around the method by which this phenomenon should be approached, and the way in which it ought to be conceptualized. The more one wishes to remain faithful to the principles of Husserlian phenomenology, however, the more awkward one finds the task of moving into this field, central as it is to specifically sociological interests.

Indeed, how is one to account for the space 'between' individuals

without having first 'unbracketed' the previously suspended existential question?   And will not such 'unbracketing' cancel the advantages transcendental reduction might offer?   These questions are
arguably the stumbling block over which phenomenological enquiry has
thus far tried to pass without success, and possibly, without hope of
ever succeeding.   Transcendental subjectivity, the central object of
phenomenological exploration, is indeed an extra-individual entity,
but it has as much in common with the interaction space between individuals as consciousness of the Husserlian kind has with the
consciousness of psychologists or of British empirical philosophy –
that is to say, nothing at all.   Transcendental subjectivity is not
an entity which may be acted upon, generated by human action,
oriented towards, or modified by design;   in short, it is not a
reality-object.   If anything, it precedes, majestically unperturbed
and immutable, all objectifiable action.   To reach it (and reaching
it is precisely what phenomenology is all about) one has to commit
oneself to many things, of which 'bracketing away' the field on which
sociological knowledge has been mounted, is one of the most crucial.

It is true that Husserl was, at least at the later stage of his
work, acutely aware of this major weakness of his system – that which
rendered it 'incommunicado' with the most vital queries arising from
sociology and cultural studies.   It is also true that he did try his
best to redress it.   It may be argued, however, that he misunderstood
the nature of the inevitable sociological complaint.   He did next to
nothing to demonstrate the relevance of transcendental reduction to
the kind of problems sociology, the science whose object is human interaction, must come to grips with.   Instead, he attempted to show
(sacrificing a good deal of his initial, stern and uncompromising,
purity) that with transcendental reduction successfully accomplished,
one can still legitimise the idea of another human being and, to go a
step further, of a human group.

And so Husserl conceived of the problem as the need to demonstrate
a legitimate passage from transcendental subjectivity to a transcendental 'inter' subjectivity.   In Husserlian terms, such a demonstration would have been valid only if it were possible to show that this
inter subjectivity is given directly, naively, pre-predicatively
within the 'Lebenswelt' – the only source of knowledge, our life as
we live it daily and as we experience it prior to any theoretical experience.   Whatever is part of the 'Lebenswelt', is given as a mode
of 'Empfindnis' – 'being at the tips of my fingers';   lying open, here
and now;   accessible without the mediation of theoretical constructs
which are produced by science struggling to let itself loose from
'Lebenswelt', and therefore shyly concealing its origin, and drawing
the curtains of abstract concepts between man and the world in which
he already lives.   Can other subjectivities be derived directly from
this 'Lebenswelt', without invoking the 'existential' data offered by
science?   Can it be shown that other subjectivities are indeed given
in this unique pre-predicative mode of 'Empfindnis'?

What follows is as ingenious as it is unconvincing. (3) A
number of relevant experiences are naively given:   the experience of
my body ('Körper');   the experience of my soul;   the experience of
their unity (i.e., the experience that my 'Körper' is a 'Leib', i.e.
a live body, animated, active entity);   the experience of the presence
of other 'Körper', who fit the description of my body known to me as

'Leib' - I see they are alive, they move, make gestures, etc.   What
is more, they are, at the moment, exactly where I was a moment before.
It is a situation, Husserl points out, similar to that of memory:
I remember myself from a moment ago, and I experience my memory of
myself simultaneously with my experience of myself now - but this
simultaneity, being the foundation of my naive experience of community with myself which transcends time, still does not blur the
distinction between past and present.   The same applies to community with the other:  'Ichliche Gemeinschaft mit mir selbst als
Parallele zur Gemeinschaft mit Anderen'.

Experience of community with others is possible only because I
conceive of the Other as an interntional modification of myself.
This is a unique feature of the Other;  no other things are constituted in the same way.   It is only the Other, in contrast to ordinary
things, who - while being represented as an empirical person - is by
the same token represented as a transcendental subjectivity.   Hence
I extend toward the other an intentional community-like bond;  and
the bond - here comes the greatest surprise - is reciprocated.

This is, indeed, the most brittle of all pillars supporting the
laboriously built bridge which is intended to connect phenomenology
with sociology.   The elegant reasoning carried out thus far has
been phenomenologically, rather than sociologically, inspired.   It
has been constructed to show that one can remain a bona fide phenomenologist and still exempt 'the others' from 'epoche'.   So far, so
good:  the mnemonic allegory is an acceptable device in philosophical
argument of this sort.   Then, however, all of a sudden, reciprocity
springs up from somewhere, but certainly not from the same line of
argument.   Up till then it had been only 'my' intellectual activity
which led to the 'Bewusstsein' of the other;  but now the other himself begins to act.   He can (but then possibly he can not) re-
ciprocate my offer of community.   Transcendental subjectivity has
been unavoidably present from the start, stubbornly there even if
concealed.   'Inter' subjectivity, however, is constituted in an
entirely different way, subject to negotiation and perhaps controversy between more than one autonomous subject.   As Ervin Laszlo
convincingly pointed out, the very concept of 'intersubjectivity' is
'either insoluble, or spurious' and hence 'illegitimate':  Laszlo
argues that there are two sharply different types of discourse - the
realistic, to which the concept of 'inter' belongs, and sceptical,
of which 'subjectivity' is a part.

The type of meaning attaching to 'inter' presupposes
several entities, and hence realism to some extent and in
some form.   On the other hand 'subjectivity.', if taken at
its face value, means that as far as any given subject is
concerned, there are only objective contents of experience,
and not necessarily 'others' such as himself.   Thus 'inter'
presupposes the many, and 'subjectivity' connotes the one.  (4)
Radical scepticism, on which phenomenology prides itself and which it
justly considers its main claim to distinction and glory, can hardly
generate 'others' as something more than contents of experience.   As
autonomous agents 'like myself', others can be substantiated only if
an argument 'from being' - which phenomenology has emphatically dis-
avowed - is restored to its own rights.

But it is not the philosophical finesse of argument which concerns

us here.   We have followed Husserl in the hope of finding a foundation on which to buttress a cogent critique of sociology.   We have
not found one.   Husserl has little to offer in the way of exposing
the original errors of the 'science of unfreedom', preoccupied, as
he is, with showing that one can clear one's sociological conscience
without renouncing one's phenomenological faith.   This desire for
sociological respectability is so overpowering, that it goads him
into fields few sociologists would dare to enter without intense em-
barrassment.   As we saw, Husserl legitimized intersubjectivity by
postulating a reciprocated intentional bond between subjectivity and
its contents.   Doubtful as it is, it happens to be only the first
step towards sociologizing - admittedly not the strongest of Husserl's skills.   And so we learn that the 'Kulturwelt' created by
intersubjectivity (a homologue of the 'Umwelt', generated by subjectivity), has, again by analogy, all the constituting faculties of
subjectivity, and thus it generates the 'spatio-temporal nature of
humanity'.   Its ultimate product is 'Gemeingeist', an exact carbon
copy of 'mentalité collective' and central value clusters, neatly
typed this time on an allegedly phenomenological typewriter.   'Gemeingeist' sediments in the form of culture, which manifests itself
in the 'unity of ends and action' - the most prominent and distinctive feature of the ethical community, the counterpart, by analogy
again, of the ethical personality.   And finally - this is the ultimate failure of phenomenology as an abortive attempt at the critique
of sociology - society may be conceived of, without violating phenomenological principles, as a synthetic personality.   To prove it,
Husserl invokes the ghosts of Spencers, Novikovs, Lilienfields:
just as a single body is built of cells, society is built of personalities (sic!).

> Die Gemeinschaftsperson, die gemeinschaftliche Geistigkeit...ist
> wirklich und wahrhaft personel, es ist ein wesenoberer Begriff
> da, der die individuelle Einzelperson und die Gemeinschaftsperson
> verbindet, es ist Analogie da, genau so wie Analogie da ist
> zwischen einer Zelle und einem aus Zellen gebauten Organismus,
> kein blosses Bild sondern Gattungsgemeinschaft.

And so we are faced with a dilemma with no viable solution.   If
we accept the logic of Husserl's legitimation of sociology, we end
up by vindicating the least savoury of those beliefs the 'science of
unfreedom' wished us to adopt - presented, moreover, in the most
primitive of possible forms.   If, following Laszlo, we point out the
immanent inconsistencies of Husserl's logic, we are left without any
proposal at all which we can consider relevant to the task at hand:
we are reinforced in our original view, that the phenomenological
programme, if scrupulously observed, can generate no sociology.   If
anything, it is a declaration of the illegitimacy of the sociological
venture.   If we do take subjectivity seriously, the conception of
partners as autonomous subjects becomes impossible.   The concept of
inter-individual space, and the communication between autonomous
subjects become unproblematic (and offer a legitimate object of study)
only if the existence of 'other minds' is axiomatically asserted.
But then all the notorious difficulties with subjectivity, only too
well known in the history of sociology, are back again, and we are
once more at square one.   As we shall see later, the problem is by
no means a minor irritant.   The critique of sociology, currently

undertaken ostensibly under the auspices of phenomenology, emanates, in actual fact, from a different source - that of existentialist philosophy.


## THE EXISTENTIALIST RESTORATION

In opposition to Husserl, existentialists were never bewildered by
the existence of others;  this never struck them as a problem with
which one has to grapple by spinning a fine fabric of subtle philosophical categories.   The presence of others appeared to them, on
the contrary, as the primary fact of existence.   The presence of
others, communication with others, being impregnated with interaction, were all integral constituents of the self, rather than
attributes which could be added at some later stage to the self
already established and complete.   Perhaps the difference should
be traced back to the fact that Husserl on the one hand, and existentialists on the other, pursued different ends.   Husserl's preoccupation was above all noetical:  ontological questions, the problem of 'whatness', came under his scrutiny in so far as Husserl
realized that the major ontological and epistemological queries can
be given a satisfactory solution only if treated conjointly, as
aspects of one central question 'how do I know?'   In existentialism
the question of knowledge, though considered seriously, plays a subordinate role.   The guiding motif of existentialist philosophy is
provided by the search for the authentic, undistorted nature of man,
rather than the undistorted knowledge man can acquire.   And the
starting point for such a quest consists, so to speak, in 'bracketing
away' precisely those essences which Husserl wished to place at the
very centre of the philosophical enterprise.   It is existence which
constitutes the most blatant, obtrusively present, ineradicable and
'pre-predicative' reality of human-being-in-the-world.   And this
being-in-the-world entails objects - things and other human beings -
from the very start, as a precondition to all philosophizing, to
existence itself.   As in the notorious Sartrian phrase 'existence
precedes essence', it is essence which can be viewed as factitious
addenda to the primary experience submerged in the living flow of
existence.   What we, in our everyday life, as a result of long and
tormenting training, consider essence, are the by-products of an inauthentic, counterfeit existence;  a testimony to men who failed, or
were not allowed, to be themselves.   Within the field structured by
the quest for true knowledge, the presence of others could not be
taken for granted.   Without the presence of others having been taken
for granted, one could not embark on the search for true existence.
  And so all being is, from the outset, being-in-the-world, which
includes being-with-others.   Now both 'being-in' and 'being-with'
are defined as consciousness that such 'not-me' is present, irremovable, and that it presents a problem, makes a relation, an
attitude, a 'modus vivendi', inevitable.   What follows is that the
only being which can be discussed - the only true being - is the
human condition of being, that founded on reflection, and containing
the realization of the separateness of the knowing self.   'Man' is
a multi-faceted concept, which, having entailed the human body and
such relations as it conditions, might encompass more than the kind

of being which existentialists would consider specifically human.
Hence the tendency to introduce other words to stand for the specifically human way of existing ('Dasein' in Heidegger, 'pour-soi' in
Sartre), words which bring into focus the reflective mode of being
and simultaneously jettison such meanings of existence as men can
share with animate or inanimate things.   It is only for humans,
that being-in-the-world means the necessity of defining themselves
in relation to this world, drawing dividing lines between themselves
and this world, defending their self against encroachments coming
from outside, distinguishing between their true selves and the shapes
the outside world presses to imprint on them.
   The tensions between the self and the world in which the self is
immersed are therefore contained in the most elementary and universal,
pre-predicative experience.   They are not caused by a specific kind
of social relations;  nor are they created by a special type of
demand raised against the world by a historically determined personality.   They are, instead, a defining feature of the human existence as such - an anthropological-by-definition factor of human life.
If they cease to be experienced and felt as 'the' problem of man's
being in the world, it may mean only a spurious emancipation from the
inherent sufferings of the human predicament.   It may mean only
losing whatever is genuinely human in man's existence, a return of
the 'pour-soi' to the pre-human 'en-soi';  a retreat from being-in-
the-world to a state in which the previously separate and autonomous
self is sucked in and dissolved by the world outside him to the point
at which he loses his distinction; that is to say, abandons his power
to see himself as an object and his relation to the world as a problem.   The demarcation between the self and his world is, therefore,
inescapable within the limits of human existence.   The split cannot
be transcended or, indeed, overcome, without destroying the 'pour-
soi' itself.   Given the fact that the world outside the self
'exists';  that it is present as an object of reflection, as an
object for a reflecting subject only in so far as the self posits it
in opposition to himself (in this sense 'creating' his own world),
then one can indeed view the existentialist idiom as a variation of
the Hegelian motif of 'Entäusserung':  the reflected upon, the
meaning-endowed, the posited world is an exteriorization of the self.
But here the affinity ends.   The Hegelian vision of the ultimate re-
absorption of the exteriorized world by the Spirit recognizing itself
in the products of its self-alienation (the vision which 'historici-
zed' the phenomenon of alienation and endowed it with a directed
dynamics) is emphatically rejected by the existentialist philosophy.
The split is not a transient stage on the way to the restoration of
unity:  it is, instead, a synonym of being human;  an episode in the
history of Nature, an eternal state for human beings:  a state coterminous with the specifically human being-in-the-world.
   As the split is unavoidable, so is the relation with others.   As
the split is, at root, an inevitable event (by definition of the
specifically human existence), though, at the same time, an act of
will, so is the relation with others.   Man is condemned to exist
physically with others, to share with them the natural world.   But
in order to coexist with them in a specifically human way, he has to
apply his own will:  one has to choose actively the right relation
with others and actively reject the corrupt, dehumanized one.   Right

relations can be founded only on the partners' decision to remain
'pour-soi'.  As the prominent existentialist psychologist L. Bis-
wanger put it, men can understand each other only in an I-Thou relation, in the intimacy of selves rather than through a clash of
objects, or an attempt of a self to master and manipulate another,
objectified human being.  The virtual being-with-others requires a
difficult and strenuous effort to establish contact on the level
of 'pour-soi', a contact in which at no stage the other being has
been reified and posited as an object.

The other, therefore, has been awarded a double and intrinsically
controversial role as a lever necessary for elevating the 'en-soi'
up to the level of authentically human 'pour-soi', while, simultaneously, being the gravest danger and obstacle to such an elevation.
The first role is a matter of conscious effort, of active decision.
The second is a matter of the obtrusive and addictive routine of
daily life, of the escape from the 'dizziness of freedom', of craven-
ly shying from the decision to be authentically human.  The second
role is the one we all know too well from everyday life.  Others
appear to us, at first sight, as an anonymous 'they', a faceless
crowd which at one stroke deprives us of our distinctiveness and
liberates us from the painful need to choose and decide.  The crowd
- this hated monster of Kierkegaard, Nietzsche, Heidegger ('das Man')
- usurps the right, once allotted to God, to pass sentence on the
human essence, on the role to which one has to conform, and the moral
principles by which one has to abide.  In exchange it offers the
comforting feeling of irresponsibility, freedom from bearing the consequences of one's own choice, from blaming oneself for the hard-
ships of life.  As we can see, this crowd of the existentialist is
keen to satisfy both needs stemming from commonsensical experience:
the need to comprehend the nature of the outer necessity, and the
desire to shift the burden of responsibility to agents of which man
can say, with a clear conscience, that they are not in his power.
It caters, therefore, for those same yearnings to which the Durksonian society attends.  What, for Durksonianists, is the benevolent
though overwhelmingly powerful society, is the crowd for Kierkegaard,
the atrocious, stultifying herd of Nietzsche, the stupefying 'das
Man' of Heidegger, the human Hell of Sartre.  With one essential
difference, however.  For existentialists, in opposition to Durksonianism, the herd-society does not gain mastery over the self unless
invited to do so, more often by default than by a deliberate surrender.  To exercise its dictatorial power, to dilute the potentially
unique self in a homogenized crowd of exchangeable digits, this
society must first undergo the process of reification (Hegel's
'Verdinglichung'), be cognitively re-cast into an all-powerful inevitability, and ultimately articulated as the omnipotent 'they'.
In fact, society becomes a second nature, an objective reality, only
if articulated in such a way.  Only if it is cognitively appropriated as 'they' who push us around, bully, drag, and force us into
being what we have no desire to be;  only if it is permitted, in
exchange for the freedom from responsibility, to depreciate our authentic existence.  Thus to be enslaved by society is a matter of
decision, or, rather, a matter of refraining from decision.  It is
by no means an unavoidable fate of human beings.  Much less still is
it the condition of becoming one.

Existentialist philosophy seems to offer, therefore, an outright and most radical critique of sociology, while meeting sociology on its own ground, appropriating its language and its problematics, and thus suggesting a meaningful - and eventually conclusive - argument. It accepts 'society' as a reality.   But, first, it insists on asking the pertinent question of how society has become (or, rather, how is it becoming over and over again) a reality in the first place. Second, it points out that the self is a highly instrumental and active (if only by desisting action) factor in this becoming. Third, it opens the possibility of questioning and challenging social re- ality, by defining it as an inauthentic existence:  by so doing it offers a wider cognitive horizon, within which the current 'here and now' social reality can no longer claim the privileged status of the sole fulcrum of valid knowledge - the sole purveyor of 'facts'.   As we shall see later, these three proposals have sufficed to attract many a thinker disaffected with the notorious flaws of the science of unfreedom.

This being so, however, the road blazed by existentialism has proved to be as rough as the alternative it came to replace.   Having successfully resisted the reduction of human existence to the oppo- site, objectified pole, it has reduced it instead to the first, sub- jective one.   Human yearnings and motives are no longer the end- products of intractable 'social reality'; rather, social reality becomes the reified consequence of the decision (or indecision) of the self.   The direction of reduction has been turned 180 degrees, to be sure; but it is still a reduction.   With the same vehemence that Durksonians fight the 'mysterious notion of free will', exist- entialist sociologists are bound to fight the 'mysterious notion of social necessity'.   The change of direction does not detract from the intensity of the barrage.

More important, if Durksonian sociology could not adequately account for the actualizations of human waywardness and could not help but conceive of freedom as a deviation resulting from the tech- nical failure of society, existentialist sociology confronts the same difficulty when trying to account for the persistent experience of society as an obtrusive and irremovable reality, and cannot help but perceive such a feeling as a deviation resulting from the tech- nical failure within the thrust for authenticity.   Both visions, because of their self-programmed one-sidedness, leave behind an un- comfortably large residue of human experience, for which they refuse to account in any other way than as odd and unfortunate abnormalities, which one can, with right knowledge and germane effort, mitigate, if not wipe out.   Being organically unable to coherently account for human freedom, the Durksonian sociology can only declare it an illu- sion.   Being similarly unable to offer a meaningful explanation of the nature-like appearance of social reality, existentialist socio- logy is bound to employ the same artifice and declare it a phantasm.

Another consequence of reductionism is, of course, a neglect of history and the ensuing necessity to project the chosen analytical idiom on to the ontological plane, as the anthropological dimension of its postulated referents.   Durksonianism can achieve such an effect by positing the formula of its reductionism as the 'logical prerequisites' of any and all organized human community.   Thanks to this expedient, the crucial category has been securely placed on an extra-temporal plane and the cumbersome problem of the 'origin' of nature-like society has been dismissed once and for all.  It is kept at a safe distance by the hypothetical bracket in which all substantial statements of Durksonian sociology are kept: given a human society, there must be a, b, c...n.  The same effect is achieved by existentialist sociology by portraying the formula of their brand of reductionism as the defining feature of authentically human existence. Once again, the problem of history has been safely removed from the agenda.  Once again, a hypothetical bracket prevents it from interfering:  given an authentically human way of being-in-the-world, there must be a, b, c, ...n.

So, it seems, we have one form of reductionism confronting another, and the problem ultimately is one of arbitrary choice, guided solely by one's preferences or research task at hand.  In one important respect, however, the society-centred version of sociology has an advantage over the self-centred one:  it pretends to offer genuine guidance to the individual, where the existentially orientated sociology leaves much to his own discernment.  Having chosen society as the humanizing agent, Durksonian sociology is capable of discussing the problem of morality as something which, in principle, can be studied and learnt with certainty.  Having chosen the stance of an objective science, it observes, of course, strict neutrality as to the personal decision of being or not being moral.  But if the decision to be moral is taken, Durksonian sociology has no difficulty in pointing out 'how' one can be a moral being, and what it is to be moral under specific conditions.  It is precisely the opposite in the case of existentialist sociology.  In the absence of supra-individual humanizing agents, being moral is an imperative which the individual faces directly as the task he must carry on his own shoulders.  When it comes to the question, however, of how one can be sure that his way of being-in-the-world is indeed moral, existentialism, as well as the sociology it may inspire, offers no reliable guidance.  'Leading an authentic life' is the only recipe.  But this is purely formal advice.  Authenticity is by definition a thoroughly individualized concept, and, also by definition, is filled with substance only by the individual himself, after the guidance, which might have been obtained from extra-individual sources, has been pinned down as inauthentic and as such rejected.  No decision taken by the individual can, therefore, ever attain that conclusiveness which may be furnished only by an agent which one sees as unimpregnable and beyond one's control.  Having declared such an agent illusion, and debunked it as a product of morbid reification, existentialism does more than just withdraw its own judgment of right and wrong;  it denies the very possibility of discussing moral problems in terms valid to more than one self.  It seems that existentialism has effectively dispelled the shroud of appearances which passed for the moral content of human existence - but only to reveal the ultimate moral void which a genuinely human, authentic life cannot escape.

We saw earlier that the Durksonian type of sociology, while addressing the imagination of an ordinary lay member of society, endeavours to satisfy these very needs which used to be catered for by the religion of the priests.  One can similarly compare existentialist sociology to the religion of the prophets.  It contains no easy promises of releasing the tormented individual from the burden of his

responsibility.  It demystifies rather than interprets the mystery
of human existence.  The demystified existence is not, however, one
which is easy to face.  The mystified world, with all the sufferings
it may cause, does emanate a comforting feeling of false security;
when sufferings spill over the brim of the safe container of daily
routine, the mystified world can still be criticised, rejected and
challenged without putting in question the integrity and moral blame-
lessness of the challenging subject.   'They' are not only slave-
masters and prison guards.  They bring, in a peculiar package deal,
redemption together with slavery, freedom from responsibility together with the unfreedom of action.  The prophets, therefore, unlike priests, offer little comfort.  Having chased away the phantom
of 'they', the prophets point their accusing fingers at the self, now
left alone on the suddenly empty stage.  It is now the self who
remains the only and the ultimate object of self-searching scrutiny
and criticism.

It is this existentialist philosophy, with its immense demystify-
ing potential and self-imposed limitations to the practical criticism
of the world, which has served as a real inspiration for those diverse currents of the critique of sociology which trace their common
roots back to the works of Alfred Schutz.  The rubric 'phenomenological', under which those currents have chosen to describe their distinctive features, is a misnomer.  We saw that the principles of
phenomenology, if scrupulously observed, are incapable of generating
any descriptive knowledge sharing its subject-matter with what has
come to be known as sociology.  It is existentialism, taking that
being-in-the-world which entails being-with-others as its starting
point, which aspires to cover a field of study comensurable with
that of sociology.  Indeed, Schutz starts from a living world much
more densely populated than the austere transcendental subjectivity
of Husserl would allow.  The presence of others, which Husserl considered the most intricate and mysterious problem of all, is to
Schutz axiomatically unproblematic.  It is the existence of such a
complex world (the very existence of which Husserl wanted to bracket
away and, later, cautiously to re-build using non-existential elements only) which, according to Schutz (and Kierkegaard, Heidegger
and Sartre) is simply given, directly and immediately.  On the whole,
Schutz is prepared to include in the 'pre-predicative sphere' much
more of the 'interpretive relevances' than Husserl originally did -
though he constantly invokes Husserl's authority to legitimate the
non-inferential character of such relevances.  (5)  The member,
rather than transcendental subjectivity, is Schutz's central category;  which means that membership in a community which shares interpretive relevances is assigned a pre-predicative modality, is located
among the preliminary conditions of the subject's life-process.
This membership, as well as the inventory of knowledge 'at hand' it
may signify, is, by the same token, declared non-inferential.  It
is thus this 'brute fact', or 'the-immediately-given', which should
be carefully surveyed and faithfully described, but which has no
meaningful 'beyond', from which one may furnish its causal explanation.  It is true that knowledge at hand is socially derived;  but
this is an assumption without much consequence, since our life begins
to be experienced, and therefore becomes an object accessible to exploration and reflection, only when the 'social giving' of that know-

ledge at hand has already taken place.    The vernacular - this ready
made set of pre-constituted types - has already been acquired.
'From the outset' is Schutz's favourite term.    It is 'from the outset' that our world is an intersubjective world of culture, and not,
as Husserl argued, something to be laboriously constructed in order
to be known.    Methodologically, the above statement means that such
sociologizing as Schutz would permit must start from the world of
culture already appropriated and incorporated by the 'member' - just
as it must start from a society which has already acquired ascendancy
over the individual, in the case of the Durksonian brand of sociology.
    This 'intersubjective world of culture', which 'from the outset'
is ours, is a world of signification which, however, is ultimately
man-made.    Not in its entirety, to be sure.    There are numerous
assumptions and generative rules which Schutz discusses as anthropologically universal structural features of the life-experience as
such; the suggestion being that they constitute unencroachable
limits, or universal conditions, of any intersubjective world of
culture.    This tendency to climb the anthropological, extra-temporal
heights, Schutz shares with Durksonian sociology.    Both lack good
tools to deal with the historically specific because of their effort,
perhaps, to posit the historically specific as universal.    Schutz is
at his best when remaining on the level of the 'generative grammar'
of experience as such.    Even when admittedly taking a specific,
geographically and historically locatable, action as his starting
point, he tends to treat this geographical-historical specificity as
a veil concealing the universal structures of genuine interest.
Home-coming, or the Stranger, rise to the level of a-historical types.
Significantly, the 'intersubjective world of culture', in the form in
which Schutz posits it as the object of research, lacks 'from the
outset' any historical dimension.
    The main role of the intersubjective world of culture seems to
consist in furnishing generative principles which differentiate and
individualize the subjectively conceived worlds of members.    Most
cultural patterns discussed by Schutz take the form of rules of cognitive structuration, which inevitably lead to results different in
each individual case.    Classification of others into members of
'Umwelt', 'Mitwelt', 'Vorwelt', and 'Folgewelt', is a universal rule,
necessitated by the natural graduation of familiarity and accessib-
ility.    Depending on these two factors, the member takes four different attitudes to such individuals, casting them accordingly into
one of the above categories.    The formal principles of such a cognitive structuration, therefore, remain the same in every case; but
the emerging cognitive structures will be, as one might expect,
sharply different, depending on the biographical situation of the
structuring member.    As Schutz himself put it, with the substitut-
ion of another 'null-point' (i.e., another biographical situation),
meaning-reference is changed.    The same applies to one of the central categories of Schutzian sociology - 'world within reach'.    For
each member, the world within reach, the only area in which 'we' (I-
Thou) relations are conceivable, and the only area to which 'in-
order-to' motives can be reasonably applied, constitutes the kernel
of each member's reality.    But again, its boundaries will surely be
drawn differently for, and by, each member, and the territories of
such worlds as circumscribed by different biographical situations

most certainly will not overlap.   The useful concept of 'finite
provinces of meaning' supplies another example.   Every member lives
within multiple realities.   Each reality is cognitively constituted
in its own specific way, which is characterized by a peculiar cognitive style, by a consistency attained by pushing some specific elements into a 'for-granted' background, by the application of 'epoche' to
a distinct sector of life-world, and by a peculiar time-perspective.
Again, all these distinctive features combine into a number of types
which are universal, in the sense of being recognizably similar in
every member's set of 'finite provinces of meaning'.   One can describe validly for all actual and possible members what kind of cognitive style, 'epoche' etc., constitutes the province of argument, or
art, or leisure.   But, as in former cases, the way in which a member
divides the shared world into provinces, when he shifts his attention
from one province to another, are by no means necessarily co-ordin-
ated.   On the contrary, these activities of members, though operated
by the same structural principles, will lead inevitably to highly
distinct results.   The concept of 'appresentational reference',
considered by Schutz a major tool of meaning-bestowing, will provide
our final example.   Any member, confronted with a series of experiences, will assign meaning to them by combining them into appres-
enting-appresented pairs.   The context in which such pairing will
take place, and consequently the selection of pairs and the division
of roles within pairs, will all vary according to the biographical
situation of a given member;   the same tools will inevitably produce
a wide variety of meanings, even if applied to 'externally' similar
objects of experience.

To sum up, Schutz's intersubjective world of culture tends to
produce, perpetuate and reinforce the autonomy and uniqueness of
each member as a cognitive entity.   Schutz has shown admirably how
the uniqueness of members is created and continually re-created with
the same inevitability which Durksonianism ascribed to the uniforming
impact of culture.   The two incompatible testimonies of experience
have been therefore reconciled on the cognitive plane:   cast into a
shared cultural world, unable to choose it as an act of will, confronting his cultural world as inescapable reality, the member is
still (due to this fact rather than in spite of it) doomed to become
and to remain a unique individual.   It is precisely the sharing of
the same structural rules of world perception which assures the uniqueness of each experience and each individual world of meaning.

If, however, as it has been demonstrated, the worlds of meaning of
individual members are unique, communication between individuals constitutes a problem.   Indeed, one has to ask how such communication
is possible at all.   Thus far, all we have learnt about the intersubjective world of culture has pointed unambiguously toward the
monadic separateness of individual cognitive worlds.   It is now
necessary to show how, given this monadic status, members may still
form and maintain a community of meanings.

Some conditions of such community Schutz assumes as anthropologically universal.   These are common assumptions, somehow made by
all members of all communities at all times - perhaps spontaneously,
but at any rate without any visible teaching-learning processes.
They are, it seems, simple elaborations on constant and primary
features of individual, but universal, experience - though nowhere is

this surmise confirmed by Schutz himself in so many words. In the
absence of any explicit answer to the question of origin of the
'stock of knowledge at hand', one is indeed free to postulate a
variety of interpretations, reaching as far as the supposition of an
inborn, species-wide propensity to perceive the world and to organ-
ize the perception according to a set of invariable rules. Not that
the question of origin matters in the case of Schutz. The rules and
assumptions combining into the 'stock of knowledge at hand' have been
introduced into the system of Schutzian sociology as an admittedly
Kantian element. They are, in fact, nothing more than a priori
conditions of all meaningful experience, and of all meaningful communication between unique cognitive subjects.

The following are typical examples. First - the assumption that
the world consists of definite objects. This assumption is drawn
from, and continually warranted by, the experience of resistance.
Its most elementary form is the resistance of our own body, which may
fall ill, become incapacitated, or be reluctant to obey our decisions.
All perception of the world as exterior and 'real' may be seen as a
modification of this fundamental experience. Second comes the expectation that experiences are typical; that they lend themselves,
in principle, to generalizations, instead of being unique and unrepeatable; that a single experience is always a member of a larger
class of similar experiences, and that, therefore, one can learn from
one's previous experience, reasonably expecting future occurrences to
conform to the pattern already known. Next, the same expectation of
regularity extends into the sphere directly relevant to the problem
of interhuman communication: one expects cognitive perspectives to
be reciprocated by other members, the standpoints assumed by the
partners of conversation to be, in principle at least, interchangeable. In other words, reciprocated understanding of each other's
meanings is an a priori given condition of being-with-others. Instead of being an end-product of the application of an intricate
technology one must diligently learn to master, understanding is
implied in each act of communication 'from the outset'. The ideal-
ized possibility of such understanding manifests itself continually
in members' assuming, in the process of communication, their opposite
numbers' attitudes, and expecting their partners to behave similarly.
Finally, there is an a priori expectation of the congruence of standpoints. Not only are they interchangeable in the sense that each
member can 'put himself' into each standpoint in turn, but they can
be harmonized, made to complement each other, with the effect that
they may be held to simultaneously by different partners in the
conversation, without rendering the discourse incomprehensible or
condemning it to failure. Let us repeat: all those and similar
assumptions are not accepted on the strength of empirical generalizations, but deduced from the analysis of conditions which must be
met if 'being-with-others', in the sense of meaningful intercommu-
nication, is to be conceivable. These are, therefore, 'theoretical
prerequisites' of the individual's existence, much as, say, 'pattern-
maintenance' is, for Durksonian sociology, a theoretical prerequisite
of the system's survival.

Those being the general conditions of being-with-others, further
factors are necessary to attain genuine subject-to-subject relations.
Schutz disagrees with Sartre's rather gloomy view of the possibility

of transcending or eschewing reification in interhuman relations.
To Sartre, the very presence of others unavoidably compromises the
authentic uniqueness of the self.   The very awareness of being
looked upon creates uneasiness and discomfort, and limits the self's
freedom;   the self experiences himself as objectified by the other,
and is incapable of avoiding doing the same in exchange.   Hence only
subject-object relations are possible.     Schutz is more sanguine.
From many types of relations between members he selects, as particularly privileged in respect to de-reification, 'Wir-Einstellung'
(equivalent of Buber's I-Thou) relations between consociates, in which
members can indeed conceive of each other as unique subjects.   This
possibility they owe to mutual biographical involvement.   It seems
that 'Wir-Einstellung' develops in the process of prolonged and continuous discourse between members, in which all aspects of each
partner's subjectivity stand the chance of being brought to light,
so as to enable each partner to grasp in time their unique configur-
ation.   Each partner learns gradually the other's unique subjectivity by exploring, in the process of active interchange, both its
flexibility and its ultimate limits.   When genuine I-Thou relations
develop, the many veils of anonymity, which normally cover the subjectivity of the other, can be removed completely.

This possibility, even if not actualized, makes all the difference
between consociates and mere contemporaries.   The latter, though in
principle accessible to potential conversation, are not sufficiently
involved in the biography of the given member to expose themselves
in the uniqueness of their subjectivities.   They will always retain
a smaller or larger degree of anonymity;   the greater the anonymity,
the poorer the set of symptoms by which they are apprehended.   Rather than being perceived as subjects, contemporaries are conceived
as specimens of a type.   Such a type refers to them, locates them
within a member's subjective cognitive map, and triggers off the
relevant unit of a member's behavioural repertoire, but it is never
identical with a concrete other.

There is, therefore, a difference in kind between the subject-to-
subject and merely typified relations.   The first are an integral
element of a member's being-in-the-world;   they are in fact coterminous with his existence itself.   The second, however, are only
of a hypothetical character.   When we speak of social relations
between mere contemporaries, what we mean is just a subjective
chance that the reciprocally ascribed typifying schemes and expectations will be reciprocated, i.e., used congruently, by the partners.
This remains a subjective chance all along, and, in so far as they
continue to be founded on 'Ihr-Einstellung' only, cannot rise above
the level of mere hypothesis.   Only that sector of the world which
has been highlighted by the biographical situation, is constantly
put in question by the members and is subject to intensive exploration.   Contemporaries, unlike consociates, are placed outside that
sector.   Untouched by the cognitive interests of the member, assigned little or no topical relevance, they - even if, in principle,
questionable - are left unquestioned.   The very phenomenon of
'type' consists in drawing a demarcation line between the explored
horizons of the topic at hand and the rest of it, which the member
leaves unexplored.

'Personal ideal types', which refer to aggregates of contemporaries (or, for that matter, predecessors or successors – who, however, differ from contemporaries in that they cannot be made partners of discourse), are typifications of the first, lowest level. There are, to be sure, typifications which are more complex, but they are always derived from those of the first-level through analogy or conflation.   State, people, economy, class – are all characteristic examples of such complex types, which we tend to treat as if they were personal types 'sui generis'.   In fact, they are abbreviated descriptions of highly complex systems of interwoven personal types of the lower order.   Because of their derivative nature, they magnify all the weaknesses of the original typification and widen the areas left in the shade and smugly taken for granted in the process of typifying.   In particular, the hypothetical nature of such types of the second order is considerably intensified.   So much has been taken for granted in the process of their typification, that the question of their verification can hardly be put on the agenda.   To depart, for a moment, from the universe of discourse designed by Schutzian vocabulary, we can say that, for all practical purposes, concepts like society or class enter the life-world of the human individual as myths, sedimented from a long and tortuous process of abstraction of which the member himself lost control at a relatively early stage (in fact, with his first step beyond the cosy realm of I-Thou relations with the close circle of consociates).

These are, it seems, the ultimate limits of the critique of sociology which can emanate from the existentialist inspiration.   Such a critique can account for supra-individual phenomena only as mental concepts.   Any critique of such concepts will consist in demonstrating that they have been arrived at by a series of mental operations subject to purely cognitive rules;   in showing that, given those rules ineradicably present in the stock of knowledge at hand, the generation of types is inescapable.   These types return later to the life-world of the individual, admitted there on the strength of analogy with personal relations – the only ones which are directly and fully experienced.   The same mental mechanisms, so to speak, de-reify consociates and reify all the rest of the individual's world – reification being itself a mental process, which consists in assuming the 'objective existence' of what is, in fact, a complex conceptual product of sifting the limited personal experience.   Schutz – and his followers with even more zeal – ascribe to such conduct the status of hypostasis:   a common logical error of imputing real referents to abstract words.


## 'SECOND NATURE' VINDICATED

If, therefore, Durksonian sociology tries hard to 'demystify' individual freedom, its Schutzian critique, apparently, attempts to 'demystify' society.   It does little, however, to assist the individual, allegedly emancipated as a result of such demystification, in acquiring practical freedom from the product of his own reifying capacity.   On the contrary, Schutzian analysis convincingly demonstrates that reification, and hypothetical types replacing the intimate, I-Thou experience of others, are built into the very fabric of the member's existence.   They can perhaps be re-negotiated and re-

made, but in one form or another they are there to stay forever.
In a sense, reification of the limited experience into the all-
powerful, though hypothetical concepts which, in turn, structure the
individual's experience, is as anthropologically universal and inevitable as Durkheim's 'conscience collective' or Parsons's, system's
prerequisites.   No room has been left for the supposition that in
some conditions reification might be avoided, that in some situations
people might be able to 'see through' the totality of their social
entanglements, and that, consequently, the Schutzian subtle analysis
of the life-world as such is just an unduly generalized description
of a specific, historically generated world.   With all its powerful
critical potential aimed at sociology, conceived as the science of
unfreedom, the Schutzian alternative refrains from offering a conceptual standpoint from which a critique of social reality (as opposite to the critique of its image), could be launched.   In this
respect it belongs to the same class as Durksonian sociology, which
it so ably criticizes.

The Schutzian existentialistically inspired system is, therefore,
specifically a critique of sociology, and not of its object.   As
such a critique, it does offer a harmoniously coherent programme
complete with a multitude of eye-opening insights.   The Schutzian
system may be conceived of as an anthropology (rather than a sociology) of knowledge, focussing its lenses on precisely those sectors
of knowledge which form the chosen domain of sociology.   Schutz has
convincingly shown that sociology, far from grasping so-called
'objective social reality', in actual fact is a once-removed modification of commonsense;   that it takes as its object not 'objective
phenomena', but products of typification, and, in consequence, per-
petuates and re-affirms the reifying tendencies of commonsense,
instead of exposing them for what they are.   Being mere products of
objectivation. 'objective phenomena' are embodiments of subjective
knowledge of 'lifewordly events'. (6) Ascribing to them any other
existential modality means perpetuating that illusion whose exposure
is the prime task of the scientific investigation of the life-world.
State, class, etc. - if they confront the individual as irremovable
constituents of his life-world - reach such a status only because
'the positing of objectivations done by one person and their interpretation done by the Other occurred "at the same time"'.   The task
of sociology consists, therefore, in unravelling the hidden mechanism
of the process of collective objectivation, which opens itself to the
eyes of an ordinary member only in the form of its end-products.

But at this point the Schutzian critique of sociology stops.   If
all we do is follow faithfully his pattern of exploring the logic of
objectivation, sociology will be stood on its feet again.   Instead
of vainly attempting to grasp social reality, we shall show more
sense in turning our attention to the structure of the process which
generates our belief in such 'reality' - starting from the only certain knowledge given to us unproblematically, i.e., knowledge der-
ivable directly from the world of everyday living.   That will be
equal to returning 'to the roots', and the Husserlian postulate 'zu
den Sachen selbst' will be fulfilled.   Schutz does not ask sociology to be critical of its object.   He invites it only to be critical of its own knowledge of that object and of the way it has arrived
at such knowledge.   Indeed, exactly like his Durksonian opponents,

Schutz precludes a priori, by sheer methodological decision, the
very possibility of the object-directed critique.  If, to paraphrase
Anselm L. Strauss, (7) Durksonian sociology assumed that the observer
(sociologist) 'has knowledge of the end against which persons are
matched', Schutz pretends to know 'the basic rules on which variations (of a personality) are composed': to know, that is, in the
sense of excluding the possibility of such rules, and not just their
applications,from ever changing.

With tough, nature-like social reality reduced analytically to
typifications and typifications alone, the question remains whether
men can ever eschew such typifying activity.  No such possibility is
left within the Schutzian system.  By explaining away the totality of
'social reality' by the most elementary and universal process of reification of meanings, Schutz depicts, first, the experience of unfreedom as the eternal, anthropological feature of human-being-in-the
-world;  and second, portrays all unfreedom as essentially alike
stemming from the same essential human endowment.  The supposition
that some elements of experienced 'reality' are redundant and can be
disposed of, that those elements derive from more restricted (and
less inevitable) causes than universal propensities of all mankind -
cannot be seriously posited within the Schutzian perspective.  But
it is only with such a supposition that the critique of sociology may
turn into a critique of social reality itself.  From Schutz's devastating vivisection of sociology, social reality emerges intact and
invincible - reduced to a benign, intellectual substance, but no less
unavoidable and overwhelming than Parsons's methodologically postulated system.

Both attempts to account for the human experience monistically,
therefore, seem equally disappointing.  Curiously, while trying to
prove that the other pole of the apparently dual experience is only
imaginary, both are incapable of questioning the necessity contained
in the first one.  Both attempts are, therefore, organically un-
critical of society, or the human predicament they describe.  The
one advantage of existentialist sociology over its Durksonian counterpart consists in its capacity to criticise knowledge in general, and
commonsensical knowledge in particular - one ability which Durksonian sociology is conspicuously lacking.  But its is a barren critique of knowledge, in the sense that it does not, and cannot, take
one decisive step further, into the critique of society, or the human
condition, itself.  We may well suspect that no fundamentalist reduction, whatever its direction, can generate such a critique.

For this reason the few theories which did attempt to avoid the
traps of unilateral reductionism deserve particular attention.  One
of them is the theory of George Herbert Mead, which drew heavily on
the world view of John Dewey.  The starting point of that theory, in
Horace M. Kallen's formulation, was 'the recognition that the first
and last 'reality' is flux, process, duration, eventuation, function,
and that ideas of unmoving substance and eternal forms are themselves
changing ideals based on passing arrests, and movements of aversion
and negation'.(8)  Mead's is perhaps that sociological view in which
existentialist dialectics have reached their furthermost limits.
Mead refused to assign unilateral priority to either of the two poles
of the most haunting of sociological dilemmas.  Instead, he brought
into focus the dialectical process of the continuous struggle and reconciliation between them, as the true starting point of sociological

analysis.   What warrants, in our view, the classification of this
solution as existentialist, is the location of that dialectic within
the subjective horizon of the self, and taking the existential predicament of the individual as the only source of data and object of
analysis.

For Mead, neither of the poles - self and society - can be reduced
to the other.   Instead, they are both present, as partly autonomous,
partly co-operating factors in every unit of experience.   Even if we
conform to the methodological rule that subjectively given information
is the sole legitimate ground for sociological analysis, we can still
without postulating entities alien to primary experience, account for
the tough, objective elements of existence, and posit them as its
projections.   Social reality is present in the most individual experience from the very start - not as a self-imposed, factitious
constraint, or an inaccessible 'other side', as in some existentialist writings.   It is visible from the subjective perspective, as
the organic ingredient of the acting self as such.   Both aspects of
the self - the notorious Meadian 'me' and 'I' - already contain objective social reality, however unique and subjective they may
appear;   though, to be sure, social reality enters each in a different way and in a specific form.   'Me' and 'I' are two aspects of
the self;   but they are also the two aspects of social reality into
which each individual is born and which he confronts in any of his
acts.   His 'I' is nothing but a lasting sediment of all previous
acts to date in which the individual has faced reality as an immediately present, situational limit to his freedom;   thus it contains society, though in a processed, individualized form, unlike
the 'me', which is reality with its face uncovered, reality in this
very moment, still 'sticking out' as an unassimilated, external
factor of the action.   The confrontation between 'me' and 'I',
which the individual experiences in each of his acts, is but the
subjective reflection of the dialectic of 'situation' and its individual 'definition'.   However we look at it, it is always the same:
the-already-assimilated against the-not-yet-assimilated reality, or
the-already-accomplished, against still-open-ended, self.   What we
conceptualize as 'society' or the 'subjective self' are, therefore,
two gigantic screens on which we project, with equal right but equally misleading, the only existential reality which is directly given
to the individual's experience:   the dialectical tension of the
social act.   Both self and society are subsumed under this act, and
only from its perspective can they be studied properly.

It is only when looked upon from the standpoint of a single act,
that the 'I' and the 'me' face each other as independent entities;
as, respectively, seats of freedom and unfreedom, impulse and its
limitations, the self's drive and its external constraints, individual uniqueness and the uniformizing pressures of a socially founded
and guarded 'role'.   When seen processually, as interwined aspects
of a biography, they lose their identity, merge into each other,
reveal their relativity and ultimately dissolve into the endless
series of the individual's on-going action-in-the-world.   It is
true that we experience intrinsic impulse as the unfinished, open-
ended, programmatic component of the situation, in which the other
component, which we call 'social reality', 'structural constraints',
or 'me', look very much like an inflexible, closed cage which arbit-

rarily cuts the trajectory of our flight.   But this truth holds only
as long as the horizon of a single act is not transcended.   From a
wider perspective, such as that of the biography as an on-going process, both look remarkably alike.   Indeed, they are, in equal measure, both open-ended and closed, both unfinished and accomplished,
temporary and conclusive.   Whatever difference we sense in their
modality-for-us has been granted by the structuring capacity of the
act at hand.   It is past situations which project present definitions.   As to the truth, however, of the reversal of the above statement, Mead was much less explicit.   We do not know - in fact, we are
incapable of knowing - whether, and in what way, the definitions of
today sediment into situations of tomorrow.   This part of dialectics
has been left barely touched.   It has been by-passed rather than
tackled in the facile W.I. Thomas adage of the truth which emanates
from the supposition of truth.   If, however, Mead is specific and
convincing in elucidating the actual mechanism of situations-becoming
-definitions, there has been no comparably strong case presented for
the other side of the dialectics of self and society.

This uneven distribution of emphases should not surprise us.   In
a truly existentialist mood, Mead attempts to disentangle the myster-
ies of the individual's existence which is always given, ready-made,
and established the moment the individual begins to reflect upon it
and thereby 'finds himself' in it.   The process which led to the
establishing of the 'outer fringe' of existence is not, therefore, a
part of the individual experience of this existence; it cannot be
surveyed 'from within', it is not opened to scrutiny as clearly and
immediately as the existence itself.   It can be reconstructed, or
rather postulated, by theorizing and abstracting, but never experienced with the same obviousness with which the other side - the subject-
ivation of the objective - is.   The aim of such theory is to satisfy
human curiosity about the 'origin' of his world, rather than lending
intelligibility to the message already contained in the experience.
One cannot preserve the purity of the method and, at the same time,
ascribe to the problem of the origin of objective reality the same
epistemological status one gives to the question of the subjective
appropriation of objectivity.   Starting from existentialist assumptions, Mead went as far as it is humanly possible toward transcending
the opposition between self and society and attaining a unified
account of an apparently polarized experience.   But the same assumptions set an unsurpassable limit to his achievement.   The dialectics
disentangled within Meadian sociology inhered in the relationship
between the ever-becoming self and a ready-made society.   To expose
the dynamics of the self, Mead had to leave in semi-shade the dynamics
of society.

Though admittedly taking inspiration from Mead's work, Berger and
Luckmann (9) have gone a long way towards transcending that limitation.   By so doing, however, they have sacrificed a good deal of the
methodological purity and cohesion of the original.   Like Mead,
Berger and Luckmann attempt to disentangle the dialectics of freedom
and unfreedom, the acting self and the limits to his action.   But
their attention is drawn in the first place to the problem cast by
Mead to the background of his central project.   Berger and Luckmann
(the telling title of their book makes it clear) wish to discover the
mechanism of the construction of reality rather than the self.

They accept, as other existentialist critics of sociology have
done, that whatever happens to man or in man - indeed, the very
process of becoming man - takes place in the presence of the world,
in the course of man's interaction with his environment perceived as
the situation of action.    Several additional assumptions are, however, introduced in the process, which purport to facilitate the ex-
plication of such presence - which other existentialist sociologies
rarely bother to elevate from the status of the 'taken-for-granted'.
Thus, we have the tacit assumption of some regularity, the constancy
of environment, which in a Homans-like fashion leads to the 'habituation' of behavioural patterns.    Frequently repeated action stops
to be problematic, is no longer an object of active pondering and reflection, and quietly moves into the field of 'taken-for-granteds',
where it becomes undistinguishable from other objective realities.
If the habituation of A's actions is now reciprocated by a parallel
habituation of B's behaviour, a new quality emerges:   habitualized
actions become typified, that is, nomically attached to typical situations.    And another assumption:   such actions tend to be selected
for typification - i.e., become institutionalized - which are 'relevant to all' actors who share a given situation.    Once institutionalized, the typified actions are reflected back into individuals'
consciousness as objective, inevitable, unavoidable, etc.    Knowledge of 'society', which emerges in such a way, is therefore a
'realization' in a double sense:   it is an apprehension of social
reality as 'reality', and, at the same time, the production of this
reality, in so far as individuals, taking its objective nature for
granted, on-goingly act toward perpetuating and continually re-creat-
ing its objectivity.    It is this knowledge which lends institutions
the appearance of cohesion and harmony they enjoy;   the order of the
universe is in the eye of the beholder, and in the habituated action
of the actor.
    This is, clearly, a revealing insight.    The idea that there is
only as much of the social order as there is of repetitious, routinized human action, and that there is no more 'necessity' in such an
order than that on-goingly generated by routinized action and the
knowledge which accompanies it, has a genuinely emancipating effect.
It means a decisive step on the road leading from the critique of
sociology to the critique of society.    It reveals the partisan,
committed nature of social knowledge, which endows the current routine (which can invoke for its legitimation nothing but a historical
coincidence) with cognitive validity and normative dignity.    It exposes the selective nature of such knowledge:   it must be selective
in the sense of suppressing information and values which explode the
security of a closed universe.    A necessary complement of knowledge
is therefore 'nihilation' - a machinery aimed at liquidating conceptually that which lies 'outside' the universe:   if socially distributed knowledge validates current reality, the mechanism of nihilation
tends to deny the validity of alternative realities and such interpretations which may relativize and put in question the existing one.
Once established, the knowledge-reality mix tends to perpetuate itself.    It acquires the power of producing reality.    And so there is
no 'social reality' unless produced by routinized human conduct;   but
there will be no routinization of conduct unless supported by the
knowledge-reality mix:

To have a conversion experience is nothing much. The real thing is to be able to keep on taking it seriously, to retain a sense of plausibility. This is where the religious community comes in. It provides the indispensable plausibility structure for the new reality. (10)

But in the form in which it has been introduced and argued for, the above idea leaves the door to the critique of society only half-open. To start with, all members in society carry an equal share of 'responsibility' for the perpetuation of the social order. Order's stability rests ultimately upon their tacit agreement to behave in the habituated way. The order, in principle, can be reduced - without residue - to the institutionalized routine of a multitude of individuals. It has no other foundations but this routine: no structure stands out from the flat plain of evenly dispersed knowledge as a solid fulcrum of societal stability. The drama of the social construction of reality is, from beginning to end, played on the intellectual stage. Members of society appear on this stage only as epistemological entities, the rest of their attributes being irrelevant and therefore not invoked as explanatory factors. Having been built entirely of thought, institutions seem to possess no more toughness and solidity than thought usually does; or, rather, thought, being the building material, lends its pliability to the entire edifice. It will be difficult to prove, within this idiom, that in the process of construction there may be points of no return, structures which acquire a new quality, sediments which cannot be dissolved simply by the re-form of meanings.

A second point is closely associated with the first: while the observation, that the existence of society consists in continuous structuring rather than in a once-and-for-all established structure, is a powerful insight from which to start a devastating critique of sociology, it suggests, in a truly Enlightenment manner, the identity of the critique of sociology and the critique of society.

It reduces the task of criticizing social reality to the critique of social knowledge. Whatever there is of 'social reality' in the human condition depends at each particular moment, 'on-goingly', upon the persistence of the meanings which members of the society attach to it. One is inclined to conclude that, were the reflective consciousness of individuals, who lend visibility of logic and congruence to social institutions, abruptly stopped or turned the other way, social reality itself would dissipate or change its content. The situation which an individual confronts as the limitation of his action is nothing more than somebody else's definition, with a shared symbolic universe as a linchpin connecting the two. No other means are necessary to perpetuate a given set of institutions, than mythology, theology, philosophy, science - and no other elements of the social world need to be re-made to replace social reality by a new one.

Third and most important - Berger and Luckmann's view of the social construction of reality begs the question of the relevance of institutions to individuals' interests by a simple assumption that precisely this relevance is the factor operative in the typification of habitual actions. To be sure, it is not clear what is the meaning which the authors attach to the last statement. The 'typification of the relevant' hypothesis may be seen as an 'origin myth', in which case it deserves precisely that measure of respect and attention those myths normally do.   It may be seen, on the other hand, as a concealed definition of relevance.   In that case one should not be misled by its pseudo-empirical form, but take it for what it is - a methodologically convenient tautology;   but then the question of why some habitual actions and not others become eventually institutionalized remains unanswered.   If, however, Berger and Luckmann mean literally what they apparently say, the doubt immediately arises whether the individuals, for whom specific actions have been institutionalized, and those individuals for whom such actions are 'relevant', are the same people.   It seems that precisely in the space stretched between those two distinct categories of individuals the problem of social reality is accommodated:   as it were, the very experience of social reality stems from the feeling of discrepancy, or incongruence, between institutions and relevance.   But this space is absent from Berger and Luckmann's vision;   it has been eliminated, from the start, by an assumption which disposes of the possibility of a critique of social reality as a problem separate and different from the critique of knowledge.

Having said all this, Berger and Luckmann's remains a bold and fateful stride towards social knowledge which, unlike the Durksonian science of unfreedom, is capable of turning into a critique of society.   Such a critique will have to embrace, as its condition and starting point, a thorough analysis of the social origin of knowledge Berger and Luckmann-fashion.   But, to be sure, it will incorporate such a critique only as its starting point.

# Chapter 3

# CRITIQUE OF UNFREEDOM

## TECHNICAL AND EMANCIPATORY REASON

Both sociology and its critique, as described in the last chapter,
admit one commitment alone: a commitment to truth, understood,
roughly, as the task of describing things 'as they really are', and
thereby of supplying a firm foundation for action. Whatever other
commitments sociology or its critique may enter into (and we have
traced a number of them), they are not part of the design and are
certainly not consciously allowed to interfere with the strategy of
cognition. Such commitments are reached unwittingly, by selectively
illuminating one or another aspect of the multi-faceted human condition. They are not consciously sought; when discovered (and they
are discovered only when a critical stance has been taken) they are
exposed as evidence of immaturity or failure of knowledge or as a
sign of its misuse. Even then they are portrayed as simply departures from the truth; in most cases, extra-scientific commitments are
carefully avoided even when those commitments already disclosed are
criticized. There is a tacit agreement between the critique of
sociology and the object of its criticism - an agreement which both
sides are eager not to transgress - to assign to the 'true description of facts' the role of not just the supreme, but the only arbiter
of their debate. Instead of exposing the many virtual commitments
of social knowledge, the debate, however vehement, reinforces social
scientists in their dedication to the pursuit of such a noncommittal
truth; and in their belief, that such truth would be accessible if
only the method of attaining it were sufficiently purified of earthly
pollutants.
   To such a programme of uncommitted knowledge the name of positivism, in one of its many meanings (the 'ecstatic purification of
passions' - Habermas), has been attached. If the programme of
positive science simply calls to investigate facts in an impartial
manner - as they really are, rather than as they ought to be or as
they could be if not prevented - the programme of positivism main-
tains that, first, the kind of knowledge which can be obtained by
positive science so organized is the only valid one, and, more importantly, that such knowledge will be, inevitably and unproblematically, as impartial and non-partisan as the attitude of the scient-

ists who produce it.   As Habermas pointed out, (1) the possibility
of such a programme was contained, though in nuce only, in the Enlightenment accolade of Reason as the supreme value and guide of
human practice in the world.   Reason was advanced by 'les philosophes' as the conqueror of dogmatic prejudice, at which door the
blame was laid for the oppressive physical and spiritual slavery men
had suffered for the greater part of their history.   In the mind of
'les philosophes', it was clearly a committed, embattled reason,
totally immersed in the most topical, urgent, and poignant human
yearnings.   The cause of human emancipation was the basis of the
case for the advancement of Reason.   The triumph of Reason over prejudice was indeed seen as that emancipation itself:  the acquisition
of knowledge, so 'les philosophes' hoped, will give men control over
their lives and destinies:  there will be no mediation between pri-
vately appropriated knowledge and private control, no by-products, no
'cognitive pouvoirs intermédiaries', no institutionalized ossificat-
ions which will rise, as unsurmountable and opaque barriers, between
man and his fate.   'Les philosophes' did not know, and could not
know, that the advancement of technically expert, instrumentally
efficient knowledge would, sooner or later, bind men to a huge artificial world on which they will depend materially but which will
not depend on their capacity to penetrate and embrace it spiritually.
'Les philosophes' did not suspect that the Reason they advanced
would coagulate into a new bondage which technically orientated science would be able only to reinforce, and which would put on the
agenda a fundamental re-thinking of the type of knowledge man will
need to control their fate.   One can hardly blame 'les philosophes'
for this failure of prevision.   They articulated the programme of
emancipation in the only terms the experience of their age had supplied.   Positive science, engaged in a mortal battle against dogmatic prejudice, was the only name available in their age for Reason
committed to the task of human emancipation.

Positivism fed precisely on what had been the historically limited,
temporary, transient form of the Enlightenment call to arms.   It
duly sifted the form from the content it was designed to serve.
Means were zestfully promoted to the rank of autotelic ends.   The
commitment to emancipation, the practical involvement which supplied
the fuel with which to launch Reason on its spectacular orbit, was
allowed to recede slowly into the background, where it could be
scanned only on ceremonious occasions, but rarely looked back to in
daily routine.   Imperceptibly but unavoidably, the commitment as
such came to be identified with a morbid departure from the chosen
path believed to lead to the only truth worth its name;  as a re-
nascence of the same dogmatic prejudice, which the pursuit of positive truth was aimed to vanquish.   Among the extra-scientific commitments lumped together in the condemned field, room was soon found
for any commitment to human emancipation which looked beyond instrumentally orientated positive science for a more powerful leverage of
human freedom.

The essential difference between the Enlightenment and positivist
Reason was that between open-endedness and closure, between the hopeful postulate and conservative description.   For 'les philosophes',
Reason was - to paraphrase Santayana - a knife with its edge pressed
against the future:  a programme of the struggle to come, aimed

against the prejudice, the ignorance, the dogmatism incarnate in
slavish obedience to the present and through the present to the past,
from which it descended.   They saw Reason as an errant knight of
virtue who had boldly, perhaps even recklessly, challenged the overwhelming powers of unreason congealed in human bondage and terror.
It was unreason which had been fortified in the trenches of human
reality 'here and now'.   To chase it away from there, Reason had to
be critical of human reality, to consider it from an autonomous perspective, to assume the standpoint of a better reality yet-to-come;
to be, in other words, willingly and consciously ideal-committed,
utopian, iconoclastic.   All these proud self-designations positivist
Reason turned into invectives.   From its vantage point they became
attributes of unreason which Reason has the task of destroying.   If
the modality of the future is one characterized by freedom coupled
with uncertainty, while the modality of the past is marked by the
blend of certainty with unfreedom – one can say that Reason, cast by
Enlightenment in the 'future' mould, has been re-cast by Enlightenment's positivist heirs, into the mould of the past.

   The stunning transmogrification of Reason on its way from the
Enlightenment to its positivist heirs holds, in fact, little mystery.
It was just one more case of the only too well known rule, whose manifestations can be easily observed whenever a utopia 'grows into'
reality:   what it irretrievably loses in the process, is its critical
edge.   Holbach could, without many qualms, subtitle his major work
'Laws of the physical and the moral world' – not because he was unaware of the distinction between facts and norms, but because (a
circumstance some wish to forget) the common denominator, which he
invoked to legitimize the conjunction, was not 'objective reality',
but reason.   It was Reason which made sense of spelling out physical
and moral laws in one breath.   In part – in the physical world –
reason had already identified itself with reality thanks to the fact
that Nature did not require any human informed mediation to 'be at
one with itself', to conflate its potentiality and its actuality.
Having dissolved itself in the works of Nature, Reason could be just
'read out' from there.   The enhancement of Reason and learning the
facts of Nature was, admittedly, one and the same activity.   In the
moral world, however, Reason resided only as a potentiality, a postulate, as a commandment, as a utopian programme for the future, still
waiting to be embraced by enlightened men and turned into reality.
The committed, value-informed practice in the ethical realm was,
therefore, the natural companion and equivalent of the unbiased,
impartial study of Reason incarnate in non-human Nature.   Were a
positivist to have furnished his book with Holbach's subtitle, he
would certainly have inserted another meaning into the same conjunction.   The physical and the moral world would, for him, belong to the
same class, not because they both are or should be subjugated to
Reason, but because both are reality, waiting to be studied in the
same impartial, detached and disinterested fashion.   But then in its
positivist incarnation Reason declares its lack of interest in human
unfulfilled potentialities and its inability to discuss them:   it is
only there that facts and values part their ways once and for all.
With Reason forced to abdicate rights to criticize and relativize
human reality, men are bound, willy-nilly, to seek levers of their
emancipation elsewhere.   But this 'elsewhere' has been condemned

from the outset as the domain of error and prejudice, variously
called partisanship, ideology, utopia.   Once the weapon of emancipation, Reason has been turned into its opponent.   The more it
succeeds, however, in disowning and disavowing the efforts of emancipation, the less challenged is the rule of charlatans and witch
doctors over the intractable human quest for a better world.   The
question is, therefore, whether Enlightenment Reason still contains
a message which can be retrieved to inform the task of human emancipation in the age shaped - materially and spiritually - by scientific civilization;   whether, in other words, Reason and Emancipation,
by now long divorced, can be brought together again;   whether Reason,
enriched but changed by two centuries of scientific explosion, can
now revindicate its critical power and the potency to inform human
emancipation.

The very success of the positive sciences, the tremendous increase in the technical-instrumental capacity of mankind, has manifested itself in the emergence of a technological civilization, which,
constructed of highly specialized and autonomous units, has detached
·itself from its source:   from the informed, goal-directed human
activity;   and which does not require, for its survival and growth,
to be penetrated in its entirety by human consciousness and reflected
in universally distributed knowledge.   It has become, therefore,
'like' nature, in the sense of being independent of human knowledge
and conscience - at least such knowledge and conscience which reflect
directly upon it as a totality, in order to guide its activity.
Positive science, contributing to expert technical-instrumental skill,
can only add further bricks to the cognitive wall which separates the
autonomous system of civilization from men who are increasingly dependent on it for their existence.   Positivism, struggling to assure
for such a science the position of monopolistic knowledge, perpetra-
tes human dependence further still, by branding with infamy all attempts to render the wall penetrable to the human eye.   It seems,
therefore, that the interest of human emancipation, the desire to
consciously control the course of human history, may not be properly
served if the positivistically informed cognitive attitude retains
its monopoly.   In Haberman's words:

this can only be altered by a change in the state of
consciousness itself, by the practical effect of a theory
which does not improve the manipulation of things and of
reifications, but which instead advances the interest of
reason in human adulthood, in the autonomy of action and
in the liberation from dogmatism.   This it achieves by
means of the penetrating ideas of a persistent critique .

The question is, however, how such a critique can render itself legitimate within the civilization informed by the ascendant positivist
idiom.

Once again, as in the times of the Enlightenment, the reason which
purports to be critical and thereby to assist and advance the process
of emancipation, has to confront commonsense as its most powerful
adversary.   With commonsense reflecting the lack of autonomy which
defines daily existence, it is reason, aspiring towards adult responsibility and the liberation of human action, which is liable to
ridicule and refutation on the grounds of evidence.   There is little
in commonsensical experience which may warrant hope.   On the contr-

ary, the totality of daily routine seems to expose its naivety and discredit its promises.   Emancipatory reason, from the outset, is denied the benefit of unorganized, spontaneous evidence comparable with that enjoyed by commonsense.   It appears therefore unfounded, rootless, crippled by all those frailties which commonsense, articulated in positivism, posits as the most odious of sins knowledge may commit - fantasy, utopianism, unrealism.   Indeed, to legitimize its claims, this reason must reach beyond commonsense and challenge the very daily existence which renders commonsense so placidly, if not fatuously, assured of its righteousness.   Emancipatory reason does not simply compete with other theories, which, like the science of unfreedom or its critique, attempt only to articulate what commonsensical experience informs men about anyway.   It recklessly denies the validity of information itself, portraying it as inconclusive, partial, historically limited, as a reflection of a mutilated, maimed, truncated existence.   Its struggle is not with commonsense, but with the practice, called social reality, which underlies it. Reason proclaims reality itself to be untrue.   Its plea against commonsense is, therefore, not that commonsense errs (commonsense has nothing against being corrected; it, too, strives to be cohesive and enjoys the feeling of being at one with logic), but that it truly reports an experience which, in itself, is untrue, being born, as it is, from the suppression of human potential.   Commonsensical consciousness, so considered, is not false; but it faithfully reflects existence which belies the genuine human potential.   Hence emancipatory reason goes beyond the merely epistemological critique of commonsense.

Emancipatory reason roams into regions which its positivistic opposite number has declared strictly off-limits.   It is set upon disclosing the factors responsible for the one-sidedness, the selectivity of human experience and the 'facts' it supplies.   It assumes that the 'prejudice' 'les philosophes' fought, is not rooted in the deficiencies of human cognitive faculties.   Its roots reach much deeper, into the very structure of the human conditions.   If positivist reason meets commonsense critically on the cognitive battlefield alone, if it chastises commonsense for not being methodical enough, for drawing wrong conclusions from right evidence - emancipatory reason does not blame it for errors of judgment.   Instead, and much more painfully, emancipatory reason puts in question the admissibility of the very evidence on which commonsensical judgments are made.   It is social reality itself which renders commonsensical awareness - even when resulting from faithful, correct reflection - false.

Such an iconoclastic attitude cannot but arouse a most ferocious resistance.   If accepted, it will surely put in doubt the virtue of commonsense, frequently identified with wisdom, and detract from the strength and attractiveness of commonsensical beliefs.   It will 'denaturalize' what commonsensically passes for nature, make the inevitable a matter of choice, transform the super-human necessity into an object of moral responsibility, and force men into questioning what has been unreflectively, and often conveniently, accepted as brute, immutable facts.   It will tear to shreds the comfortingly tight protective shield which leaves so little within the reach of human decision and responsibility.   It may well render unbearable the same human condition which commonsense tries hard - and successfully - to make tolerable.

It is thanks to commonsense that man:
knows who he is.   He feels accordingly.   He can conduct
himself 'spontaneously', because the firmly internalized
cognitive and emotive structure makes it unnecessary or
even impossible for him to reflect upon alternative possibilities of conduct .... The socially available definitions
of such a world are thus taken to be 'knowledge' about it
and are continuously verified for the individual by social
situations in which this 'knowledge' is taken for granted.
The socially constructed world becomes the world 'tout court'
- the only real world, typically the only world that one can
seriously conceive of.   The individual is thus freed of the
necessity of reflecting anew about the meaning of each step
in his unfolding experience.   He can simply refer to 'common
sense' for such interpretation .... (2)

What man loses in the breadth of his cognitive horizons and in the
extent to which his inner potentialities may be realised, he certainly gains in emotional security.   He attains a deluding, but
rewarding impression of the meaningfulness of his world by severely
limiting the part of it which he expects to possess meaning.   He
acquires the ability to cope with the harsh realities of the public
world because he believes, as he is told, that he bears responsibility only for his narrow private world.   In so believing he does not
err;   his consciousness is false only 'by proxy' in so far as his
actual condition falsifies his true potentialities.   There is, in
fact, a two-way correspondence between the human situation and its
commonsensical reflection.   It is thanks to this correspondence that
commonsense is cognitively satisfying and pragmatically effective.
In this double utility it is confirmed and reinforced by that type of
social science which codifies and articulates the convenient surrender.   As Henry S. Kariel put it:

just as a dream of an iceberg floating by keeps us asleep
when our blanket has slipped off the bed, the report of
political science that apathy is a function of healthy
political system reconciles us to the exploitation of part
of the body politic.   Political scientists consolingly
reveal that whatever happens is 'really' no accident.
They disclose the existence of underlying patterns -
pattern assumed to lie in nature, imposed by Fate, History,
Rationality, or the Logic of Events.   Relying on Ein-
stein's metaphysical sentiments, they assume that God does
not play dice.   Like the great works of theology and art,
their rationalizations fill a human need:   they make our
existence tolerable.   And like the great achievements of
theology, they help implement what the powerful allege to
be the consensus.   (3)

In the struggle against the reality protected by commonsense, emancipatory reason starts off from a handicapped position, being bound
to revive the anxieties and the terrifying uncertainty of human fate
which commonsense so consolingly puts to rest or hermetically seals
off.

Unlike instrumentally motivated knowledge, emancipatory reason
does not promise to facilitate the tasks commonsense strives to ful-

fil: the tasks of making the best of the world 'given', in all its
dazzling obviousness, in the most elementary experience.   It does
not offer to assist commonsense in its effort adequately to process
and systematize the seemingly unmistakable information experience
supplies.   Instead, it comes up with a piece of advice which is apt,
if taken seriously, to pulverize the solid walls of the cosy everyday
world: it proposes, in all earnest, to take an ironic attitude toward experience itself, complete with the allegedly unshakable
'facts' it furnishes.   If commonsense asks men to believe in 'laws
of nature' which emancipatory reason finds difficult to accept, the
reaction does not confine itself to re-checking the method of commonsensical fact-gathering and the logic of commonsensical reasoning.
Inevitably, it strikes at the 'experience' which supplies such facts
and stimulates such reasoning.   It questions the 'natural' character
of the putative 'nature'.   The ironic detachment from commonsense
which emancipatory reason propounds and cultivates, has its sharp
edge turned against social reality, and not against human cognitive
or moral faculties.

It is for this reason that the critique aimed at emancipation is
bound to consider commonsense as an obstacle.   Commonsense can only
fulfil its cognitive and emotional functions to the extent to which
it succeeds in closing its eyes to 'alternative realities'.   All
the power of conviction which commonsense may carry ultimately rests
on the assumption that the reality conveyed by commonsense is the
sole reality, while commonsense is the only channel through which
information about it may be obtained: reality is one, and commonsense is its spokesman.   Commonsense, assisted by the technically
orientated science which reforges its findings into utilitarian
knowledge, spare, therefore, no efforts to expose and unmask 'false
prophets' of alternative realities.   As we have seen, the technical-
scientific idiom offers quite a few categories which have been coined
with this purpose in mind.   A 'possible reality', which is unable to
produce a certificate of viability issued by experience, is branded
unrealistic, irrational, or utopian - depending on context.   On the
contrary, emancipatory reason can claim its legitimacy only on the
condition that the one reality of which commonsensical experience
informs us has no more foundation than a historical coincidence can
give, and by no means can be considered as the only one which is
possible and conceivable.   In particular, it perceives the limitation of the range of possibilities, as signalled by commonsense, as a
mere reflection of the limitations imposed on human action by changing historical practice.   Neither the one, nor the other is final
and irreparable.   To discover alternative kinds of practice which
have been suppressed and temporarily eliminated by the unique course
of man-made history, one has first to accept them as a possibility;
and that requires a hypothetical refutation of the finality of commonsensical evidence.

Emancipatory reason is at odds with commonsense (and that technical-instrumental knowledge which shares its philosophical standpoint) in one other vital respect.   Having accepted historically
accomplished reality as the only source of legitimate knowledge,
commonsense, together with derivative science, limits its recognition of choice to that which is posited as 'decisional nods' in an
otherwise deterministic process.   Positivism denies science the

right of discussing 'ends'; indeed, this voluntary abstention from
stepping beyond the realm of means, from seeing the discussion of
values as its objective, from asking questions about the 'ends of
history' or the 'meaning of human existence' - all these aspects of
self-imposed modesty define that science which positivism recognizes
as the sole form of valid knowledge.   But the distinction between
ends and means, which delineates the limits of scientific pursuit, is
nothing but a reflection of the dividing line between things controlled and things beyond control, again, as drawn by that social
reality which has been historically accomplished.   In social life,
'means' refers to activities or their aspects which have been left
flexible and which can and should be directed by human choices.
'Ends', on the other hand, are large-scale states or changes which
are not, at least not directly, an object of deliberate decision made
by specific people.   They are located on the level of this societal
totality which gained independence from conscious, purposeful human
activity.   If men happen to become objects of such decision, science, as in the case of the Weberian charismatic overlords of means-
oriented bureaucracy, can neither interfere nor help.   As for the
historical process as a whole, its ends can be theoretically depicted
as remote consequences of minute, sectional decisions.   But they do
not figure in these decisions as 'in-order-to' motives.   They follow
such decisions in an a fortiori inscrutable way, whose logic may be
penetrated only in retrospect.

Knowledge orientated towards technical-instrumental interests has,
as it were, no tools with which to analyse and select 'better ends'.
Instead, it locates the ends inside the reality which it takes for
granted, as given, as the starting point of all inquiry.   By the
same token, such knowledge follows commonsense in implicitly assign-
ing to ends a status akin to inevitability.   They are not considered
to be a matter of choice; they are, if anything, the supreme criterion of all other, smaller, more limited choices.   Social reality is
historically constructed in such a way as to prevent some major questions from ever becoming an object of the deliberate consideration
and decision of men.   Commonsense reflects this structure of social
reality by preventing men from facing such questions as objects of
their responsibility and decision.   Instead, the life-process and
its intellectual reflections are split into a multitude of tiny and
relatively inconsequential decisions, none of which is practically or
intellectually related directly to the major dilemmas of the human
condition.   Thus commonsense presents as a supra-human necessity
what social reality has already placed beyond the realm of human
control.   In this respect, as in so many others, social reality and
commonsense support and reinforce each other.   Man abstains from
rebellion, and social reality in exchange prevents him from facing
situations which may occasion that utterly unpleasant, tormenting
feeling of incertitude.   As Voltaire's Martin would say-'Travaillons
sans raisonner .... C'est le seul moyen de rendre la vie support-
able'.

And thus, technical-instrumental knowledge has none of the tools
which would be required were one wishing to evaluate ends with the
same degree of certainty and precision with which this knowledge ev-
aluates actions defined as means.   Technical-instrumental knowledge
willingly admits its incompetence.   But, at the same time, it denies

the possibility of any other type of knowledge passing authoritative
verdicts on issues it shirks discussing.   Denied a more sophisticated methodology, and warned against ideas which might stretch its
imagination beyond the limits of reality at hand, commonsense will
obviously opt for the only ends which can produce evidence of their
'reality' - i.e., those ends which are woven into social reality itself and therefore appear to the individual as an outer necessity.
Science will then agree with commonsense that the 'satisfaction of
human needs' furnishes the ultimate, and utterly non-partisan limit
t o the field of such human affairs as may be instrumentalized and
thus judged, served and perfected by science.   But not human needs
themselves - which are just given, and which one would expect monot-
onously to remind us of their obstinate presence whatever happens in
the instrumental sphere.   What has been left unsaid is that those
needs themselves are, in the long run, a cultural, i.e. non-natural,
product (except for the few 'physiological', organic needs, whose
discussion makes, however, little practical sense, since in every
known culture they are theoretically conceived rather than appearing
in their pure, unadorned form).

It is true that until very recently human needs  entered human
relations as unarguable starting points, rather than as objects of
intentional manipulation.   They were the results of human action
none the less, albeit action uncontrolled by understanding and uninformed by anticipatory knowledge.   Once established, they enter,
in the form of expectations and demands, in a feedback relation with
social reality, which in its turn lends them some of its appearance
of inevitability.   The resulting commonsensical attitude of taking
them for granted further contributes to their entrenchment and ob-
scures even more the fact of their human, historically contingent
origin.   This means, in practice, that the chance of submitting
them to a conscious, informed human control becomes more remote still,
and the commonsense-fed positivist idiom, which denies the right of
critical reason to assess human needs, is partly to blame for the
perpetuation of this situation.   By endorsing the expedient of
splitting existential issues into a plethora of short-range, narrowly
circumscribed daily decisions, science, oriented toward technical
interest and allegedly set upon the rationalization of human action,
unwittingly propagates the irrationality of historical process -
though only by default.   To quote Habermas again:

> the root of the irrationality of history is that we 'make'
> it, without, however, having been able until now to make
> it consciously.   A rationalization of history cannot
> therefore be furthered by an extended power of control on
> the part of manipulative human beings, but only by a higher
> stage of reflection, a consciousness of acting human beings
> moving forward in the direction of emancipation.   (4)

To sum up - emancipatory reason comes into conflict with commonsense on three crucial fronts: it is set upon 'de-naturalizing' that
which commonsense declares to be human - or social - nature;   it
exposes and condemns the commonsensical dismissal of alternative
realities;   and it attempts to restore the legitimacy of those existential issues which commonsense, following human historical predicament, pulverizes into a multitude of such mini-problems as can be
articulated in purely instrumental terms.   In view of those dis-

agreements, emancipatory reason cannot settle for - truly or falsely
- correcting commonsense and enhancing its theoretical sophistication,
as does Durksonian sociology;  nor can it settle for turning its
searching lights on commonsense itself, in order to explore the
generative grammar of beliefs which commonsense presents as platitud-
ionally obvious, as did the critics of sociology inspired by existentialism.   It cannot stop short of questioning the very reality
which commonsense strives faithfully to reflect - and, therefore, of
undermining the very basis of commonsense's authority as a trustworthy
source of true knowledge.

One can point out a common denominator in all three major points
of controversy between emancipatory reason and commonsense:  that is,
the conflict between the historical and the natural perspective.
Emancipatory reason can prove its case only if it succeeds in re-
arranging experiential knowledge in terms of its truly historical
structure.   And it is precisely an in-built tendency to positing
the historical as the natural (i.e., timeless), which supplies
commonsense with its most crucial cognitive principle.   Indeed, it
is not only the first point of disagreement which makes sense only
if viewed against the background of this paramount conflict;  the
same applies to the two remaining issues of contention.   The case
for a specific social reality being unchallengeable and unchange-
able in one or another of its aspects could not be seriously upheld
were this reality assessed as historically contingent.   And the
multitude of mini-issues tend to congeal into great existential
problems immediately (and only when) the questions of their historical
origin are seriously asked and, consequently, the suspicion of their
historical transcience is solidly founded.

It is this historical perspective which allows us to transcend the
opposition between the two poles of the pre-predicative human experience (definition and situation, motives and constraints, control
and system), on which the supposedly fundamental controversy between
Durksonian sociology and its existentialist critics is founded.   Indeed, the actor's and the situation's poles of action are counter-
posed as mutually independent agents and dissonant forces only if
surveyed within the framework of a single act, or a set of identical
acts.   The autonomy of poles disappears, however, if the narrow cognitive horizons are broken, and the act begins to be seen as a link
in a historical chain.   What transpires then is the fact that the
poles are inextricably linked to each other and, indeed, constitute
each other.

What we mean here is constitution as historical process - not the
'cognitive' constitution, easily acknowledged by sociology which has
no use for historicity:  the latter is the trivial truth that the
situation and its definition are inconceivable in isolation from each
other.   Recognition of this trivial truth is in no way related to
the willingness or unwillingness to look beyond the boundary of a
single event, towards men as historical agents.   It requires only
the much simpler acceptance of the actor as an epistemological agent,
who either appropriates or posits the segment of reality brought into
relief by his intentions, motives or intellectual labours.   As we
have seen, the only form in which time and process are admitted into
this picture is the biographical past of the actor.   But such an
individualized history is too weak a lever to lift the barrier separ-

ating the two poles of action-structure;  the other, situation-
centred pole, is as autonomous toward the biography of the actor as
it is in relation to the actor's momentary intentions.

   Not so in the case of a truly historical constitution.  Here,
the juxtaposition of actor and his situation is reduced to its proper
status – a momentary snapshot of a process in which men play both of
the roles so clearly distinguished in a single act – that of subject
and object of history.  This dialectical unity of both sides of
human experience has been admirably expressed by John R. Seeley:

> What is lost from sight in this way of talking is again
> that the principle of inclusion is not 'given' (like the
> liver-cell's relation to that liver and that body in which
> the liver lies), but 'enacted';  that what is involved is
> a loyalty, not a locus;  that while there are two-way con-
> sequences, so that neither the soldiers nor the army are
> conceptually or practically independent, the relations are
> not those of logical implication (as in the parts of tri-
> angles) nor necessity (as in the body-cell), nor even un-
> dying convenience.  (5)

If they happen to be, by chance, historical relations, then the opposition of actor and his situation, instead of passing for the ultimate, pre-theoretical reality from which all investigation must start,
becomes itself an occurrence to be explained, and, above all,
questioned.  Whatever insuperable constraints the here-and-now situation may entail, will then reveal their true nature:  that of sediments of past actions and choices.


## 'SECOND NATURE' SEEN HISTORICALLY

No theory to date has gone further than Marxist sociology in elucidating the historical contingence of the allegedly natural conditions
of human existence.  Marxist sociology locates the science of unfreedom and its existentialist critics as parts of the same historically limited conditions, and thereby opens the possibility of their
creative transcendence.

   Marx's argument against Adam Smith  (6)  may be considered as a
typical example of the method of critique.  Smith, much like Durksonian sociology and its critics, 'naturalizes' historical conditions
of human existence.  Capital, prices, exchange, private interest,
etc., he sees as pre-conditions of the life-process, as 'objective
facts' from which any life-process, as well as its study, is bound to
start.  Marx questions this assumption:

> The dissolution of all products and activities into
> exchange values presupposes the dissolution of all
> fixed personal (historic) relations of dependence in
> production, as well as the all-sided dependence of the
> producers on one another.  Each individual's product-
> ion is dependent on the production of all others;  and
> the transformation of his product into the necessaries
> of his own life is (similarly) dependent on the con-
> sumption of all others.  Prices are old;  exchange also;
> but the increasing determination of the former by costs
> of production, only develop fully, and continue to

develop ever more completely, in bourgeois society, the
society of free competition.  What Adam Smith, in the
true eighteenth-century manner, puts in the prehistoric
period, the period preceding history, is rather a product
of history.

It is the individual's dependence on the anonymous multitude of
other members of the society which appears to him as 'social necessity', as the 'objective situation', against which he is bound to
measure his own motives and intentions, and which furnishes him with
the only 'objective' criteria of rationality of those motives.  But
this appearance is itself a historical creation.  It emerged at
some point in history when human sociability, 'being-with-others',
ceased to manifest itself as relations which - like personal relations - could be, in their totality, cognitively appropriated by the
individuals involved.  With the extension of relations of exchange
the net of dependence transcended the narrow field which the individual could consciously control qua individual, in face-to-face,
person-to-person, encounters.  Such encounters now became small
sectors of large totalities whose further reaches dissolved into the
obscurity of unknown and invisible dependencies.  To be properly
understood, they now had to be cognitively dovetailed into a large
network of relations:  an intellectual feat which could not be performed without theoretically constructing a model, which would render
intelligible what was not empirically accessible.  To be controlled,
they required human individuals to transcend their situation qua
individuals - the situation in which they remain in their daily routine - and consciously to revindicate their group life, commensurate
with the field of their dependencies.  And thus a gap was created
between the individual's creative and appropriating activities, between being-for-others and being-for-himself, between the individual's
self-actualizing drive and the conditions of his own survival.  The
gap is perceived as a permanent clash between private interest and
social reality.  It is to be cognitively filled by an ideology -
which, as the field of dependencies it attempts to make comprehen-
sible - must transcend the data immediately given in the individual's
daily experience.

Hence, in opposition to his primitive followers as well as to his
equally primitive and superficial critics, Marx did not reduce social
life to economics, thereby offering another version of a 'science of
unfreedom'.  On the contrary, he reduced economics to its social
content;  he re-wrote political economy as sociology, and sociology
as history.  It was only as the result of a specific, and perhaps
unique, historic development that economic dependencies gained ascendancy over all other human relations;  that they came to appear as
inflexible, objective conditions of human existence and the ultimate
limits of human freedom;  that they congealed, in other words, into
'objective social reality', a 'second nature'.  It is only because,
in order to exist, he has to move in a network of dependencies he can
neither scan nor control, that the individual has become 'privatized'
('private' is an antonym of 'public'), that he has to view his own
interest in survival as threatened and conditioned by faceless others,
whom he meets only as an oblique, inscrutable 'objective reality'.

Private interest is itself already a socially determined
interest, which can be achieved only within the conditions

laid down by society and with the means provided by society;
hence it is bound to the reproduction of these conditions
and means.
And, most importantly:
   the social character of activity, as well as the social form
   of the product, and the share of individuals in production
   here appear as something alien and objective, confronting
   the individuals, not as their relation to one another, but
   as their subordination to relations which subsist independently of them and which arise out of collisions between
   mutually indifferent individuals.
   The opacity of social institutions, the optical illusion of their
autonomy, parallels their removal far beyond the reach of commonsensical experience.   The individual's modalities of producer and
consumer are still visible from the commonsensical perspective, but
not the link which connects them.   All the vast social space which
extends and mediates between the productive effort and consumer satisfaction enters the realm of commonsensical experience only in the
form of 'exchange value' and 'money' – the first representing and
concealing the intricate web of the individual's dependence on
activities of others, the second epitomizing such power as the individual may possess over these activities.   The only information
commonsense offers in such circumstances is that given more money,
the individual may appropriate more exchange values.   The only advice
commonsense may supply, is that the individual should try, to the
best of his ability, to obtain more power (= money), in order to gain
more freedom (= exchange values standing at his disposal, and therefore subjugated and tamed).   The relations of production, exchange
and appropriation obtained the crucial, determining, nature-like role
they possess in the market-based society not because of some mythical
'primacy' of economy over the rest of social relations, but because
they, in the first place, have been withdrawn from immediate, conscious human control and therefore have become independent of those
people whose activities constitute their only substance.   They are
still nothing but the sum-total of a multitude of human interactions.
But to every single individual who partakes of these interactions
they appear as 'something alien and objective' – in a way not very
different from that in which the cat's tail appears to him as an
alien object.   Other non-economic, social relations coagulate into
power, i.e., into tough, constraining, pressure-exerting 'reality' –
only as derivatives of structures already petrified by economic
dependencies (the idea expressed in the metaphor of the 'superstruct-
ural' character of political, social and cultural powers).   And vice
versa – a type or a sector of human relations may be emancipated from
the 'iron laws of social reality' and re-appropriated by human individuals as conscious controlling agents only to the extent to which
they are independent of economy and located beyond the reach of the
treadmill of money-exchange values.   Hence the discovery, by the
critics of Durksonian sociology, of face-to-face encounters, the
narrow enclaves of inter-personal relations, as the fulcrum on which
to base human meaning-negotiating freedom.   Hence their tendency to
enclose their cognitive universe within the walls of a psychiatrist's
anteroom, a married couple's bedroom or university seminar.   If the
freedom to negotiate meanings and to actualize one's self-definition

may indeed be found in these secluded places, it is only because, and in so far as, these places, and the activities which occur there, have been disgorged or disowned by, and then securely isolated from, the 'public' sphere ruled by anonymous necessities standing for the network of economic dependencies.

The 'public' sphere enters the commonsensical experience of the individual as a nature-like, superior reality in so far as it has been removed from an immediate relation with the individual.   A new realm has been spread out between the individual creative effort (the production of utility objects by transforming natural ones) and the human life-supporting activities (which still can be seen as directly related to human will, as the realm, at least partly, of individual freedom).   This realm in fact connects the two disparate halves of the existential cycle, though, from the perspective of the individual experience, these halves appear to be short-circuited by money and exchange value.   As far as individual commonsensical wis- dom is concerned, money and exchange values stand for this mysterious, impenetrable realm into which the individual's products disappear and from which articles of the individual's consumption emerge.   But money and exchange value obscure rather than determine (much less illuminate) the virtual social character of this realm: they present social relations as economic.   The task of critical sociology is to revindicate the social substance of the social world.

In this, critical sociology differs from both Durksonian sociology and its existentialist critics.   Durksonian sociology, so to speak, takes commonsensical appearances at their face value; since they appear inevitable and irremovable, it declares them to be such and proceeds to supply us with their precise and comprehensive descript- ion.   Its existentialist critics refuse to acknowledge the reality of appearances, but first, go instead for investigating the mental process which posits them as 'reality', and - second - refrain from investigating other realities, which those appearances perhaps con- ceal.   Instead, they retreat into exploration of the individual's freedom at the periphery of the social world - exactly where that freedom has been evicted by the realities which the rejected appear- ances distort and hide.   They attempt to portray such periphery as a self-sustained world (both cognitively and morally) and, moreover, as the very centre of the life-world from which all other components of this world emanate.   Thus, they attempt to short-circuit severed halves of human existence, in much the same way as it is done by money and commodities, only using language for the work done in the social world by money (to which Marx would retort: 'To compare money with language is ... erroneous.   Language does not transform ideas, so that the peculiarity of ideas is dissolved and their social char- acter run alongside them as a separate entity...' (7)).   Critical sociology sees both strategies as well founded in the historically developed commonsense of the market society: in a commonsense which has tacitly accepted its historical limitations and therefore per- ceives them as unencroachable.   Both strategies seek to illuminate commonsense without questioning its self-determination.   By so doing, they both replicate the limitations of the commonsense they serve.

The conflict between critical sociology and the two alternative strategies is not simply the question of an ultimately arbitrary

preference, which, like taste, is not worth arguing about.   Critical
sociology shows that the alternative strategies fail, and are bound
to fail, in their attempts to inform human existence in a way which
can make emancipation possible, since they accept, as being irremovable, precisely those aspects of historically contingent reality
which render such emancipation inaccessible.   The idea that one can
tack together 'pour les autres' and 'pour soi' aspects of one's existence by an intellectual and moral effort alone, can only tempt
false hopes of illusory emancipation.   The idea will make the fiss-
ure - and the resulting unfreedom - even more immune from emancipatory efforts.
     Such an idea is an illusion, since in the market society the life-
process of the individual cannot be contained within the narrow field
of 'Umwelt':   that sector of 'the others' with whom the individual
has a chance of entering into linguistic communication - to meet
face-to-face, to stimulate to action and respond to, to bargain about
definitions of the situation and status-assignment, to negotiate
meanings, etc.   In a technologically primitive, pre-modern society,
with the circulation of the totality of goods limited to a small
circle of people belonging to cognitively accessible kinship or local
group, the itinerary of all items listed in the inventory of the
life-process remained, from beginning to end, within the sight of the
individual.   The network of dependencies overlapped, therefore, with
the network of personal relations;   dependencies were seen as oblig-
ations, and were defined by a kinship or estate category to which the
individual belonged.   It was there that economic dependencies were,
in a direct and literary sense, culturally founded;   they were coterminous with status-definitions and the meanings attached to them.
However unfree or dependent an individual was in such conditions, the
sources of his unfreedom held nothing mysterious, they were easily
ascribable to specific individuals who wielded the strings of dependence.   A powerful church and the awesome will of God were, therefore, necessary to make up for the deficiencies of social bonds too
transparent to secure their own perpetuation and to keep subordinate
groups - those offered the raw end of the deal - in their grip.   The
dependence and non-autonomy of individual life was visible from within commonsensical experience in its true nature - that of personal
bondage - and required, therefore, super-human cultural sanctions, in
the shape of institutionalized eschatology, to be sustained.   Reproduction of the economic system hinged in effect on the reproduction of the crude but easily assimilable web of cultural definitions.
     Disintegration of kinship and local ties, the shaking off of imm-
utable status definitions and their super-human sanctions, coincided
with the emergence of this unique conjunction of personal independence with impersonal bondage, which is typical of market society.
It is here that Steinbeck's hero, evicted from the land of his
fathers, feels agonized by the realization that there is 'nobody to
be shot' for his misfortune.   The blight cannot be pinned to any
particular individual;   the intricate tissue of causes reaches far
beyond the cognitive horizon of the individual, and clearly could not
be woven out of personal responsibilities and guilts.   As the web of
dependencies lost its human nature, super-human sanctions are no
longer necessary to keep it intact.   The system of dependence can
exist on its own, as a result of its opacity, impersonality, recon-

dite and inscrutable nature.    It appears now, and only now, as a
mysterious 'social reality', as a nature-like objectivity, which
must be obeyed.    Obedience, to be sure, is now not a moral act,
but a question of reason and rationality.    The individual is well-
advised not to overreach himself, not to embark on a futile struggle,
not to challenge social nature - not because that would be a morally
morbid act, a rebellion against supreme moral power, but because such
an act of disobedience will be against his own personal interests.
Hence, in retrospect, the market society appears as tantamount to
personal liberation.    The bondage once supported by fear and an
ideological lie is now willingly and 'freely' chosen for the sake of
well understood and rationally assessed personal interest.    In the
age of reason and informed choice, knowledge of the functional prerequisites of the 'second nature' is an apposite and sought-for substitute for the terror of God's vengeance.    It assumes that the
individual is a free agent;  it appeals to his reason and intelligence instead of his prejudice and fear.

   In a market society, 'the reciprocal and all-sided dependence of
individuals who are indifferent to one another forms their social
connection'.    They are indifferent to each other, in the sense that
they do not meet as persons, do not consciously interact, and may
well be unaware of each other's existence:  but they depend on one
another, for the simple reason that the precise form of the product
of one individual's activity, which returns to him transformed into
some finished article for his consumption, will depend on the activities of innumerable other individuals of whom the individual in
question has neither intellectual awareness nor practical control.
The lack of personal bond holds, of course, in both directions.
Hence the experience of personal freedom, which arises from the fact
that no other person (an individual physically, cognitively and
emotionally close enough to be perceived as a person) guides the
individual in question in his choice, far less foists such choices
upon him.    Such constraints as individuals experience while making
choices and putting them to the test, are much too inflexible and so
unmistakably beyond persuasion to be explained away as the works of
specific persons.  'Individuals are subsumed under social production;
social production exists outside them as their fate;  but social
production is not subsumed under individuals, manageable by them as
their common wealth'.    Economic dependencies now in fact do precede
and frame all other kinds of interhuman relations;  they appear, at
the outset, as the inexorable conditions of all human action and as
unsurpassable limits to freedom of choice.    But it is, Marx insists:
   an insipid notion to conceive of this merely 'objective
   bond' as a spontaneous, natural attribute inherent in
   individuals and inseparable from their nature (in antithesis to their conscious knowing and willing).    It is a
   historic product.    It belongs to a specific phase of
   their development.  (8)
The split of the elementary human experience into the willing subject and his constraining environment (the split on which all sociology is built), is therefore a result of historic development and by
no means can be taken as a perpetual, species-ascribed human condition.    This, itself, requires explanation, and the explanation is
bound to be historical.

To be fair, one has to admit that in their more inspired moments sociologists do play with the idea of the historical changeability of the human condition. But more often than not, history in their ratiocination boils down to typology, or rather to a dichotomic division of known types of social organization and, consequently, of human action. The idea appears under different names, though, given all their differences in emphasis, such variously described pairs betray a surprisingly wide range of similarities. 'Gemeinschaft' and 'Gesellschaft', military and industrial society, theological and positive eras, ascriptive and achievement societies, mechanical and organic solidarities, non-industrial and industrial societies - all these concepts, however rich their content may be, stand in fact for the same persistent realization of the antithesis between personal freedom caught in the net of impersonal dependencies (typical of market society) and the lack of personal choice combined with the evidently personal nature of dependencies (typical of a society with market undeveloped). The only alternative to the reality at hand, which the positive attitude can tolerate, is that state of affairs which has been eliminated, as a viable alternative, by the advent of present conditions. Hence history enters into consideration only in the form of a choice between two types. Disaffection with the type presently in ascendancy - if it does find its way into sociological analyses - automatically results in idealizations of the other type. Remedies for the resented partiality and inauthenticity of individual existence are sought in the allegedly 'fully developed' personality of a pre-modern society. To this Marx would retort, that 'it is as ridiculous to yearn for a return to that original fullness as it is to believe that with this complete emptiness history has come to a standstill'.

Alternatively, the same tendency manifests itself in persistent attempts to posit reciprocal dependencies as personal, and therefore manageable, in conditions where they are definitely not amenable to conscious human management. Paradoxically, this ideational 'humanization' of impersonal bondage belongs to the same category as opposite attempts to ascribe super-human status to what used to be simple and transparent personal serfdom. In their practical effects, both attempts bar or misguide actual or potential efforts of emancipation, soliciting inadequate action, or an action aimed at misplaced targets. One way of perceiving reciprocal dependencies as personal is to depict them as arising from inadequate meanings, imposed by 'the others' and distorting the true, authentic existence of the individual. This is the existentialist view of the roots of human bondage - according to which the presence of others compromises, constrains, and confounds the individual's quest for 'pour-soi', for authentic existence. Sociological offshoots of existentialist philosophy, of which Garfinkel-style ethnomethodology is a foremost example, present dependencies and constraints as sediments of meaning-negotiation, as an ongoing accomplishment of 'work', which consists of 'talking'. The appearance of social reality, of external constraints upon human freedom, is posited therefore as a cultural phenomenon, in historical conditions distinguished precisely for the liberation of the social structure from its previous dependence of cultural factors. Strange as it may seem in view of their extra-scientific animosity, there is not much difference between these attempts and the tendency of 'folk-

lore' Marxism to personalize the roots of human unfreedom, by pinning
it to capitalists, parties, governments, etc.  Here the misplacement
consists in presenting the impersonal web of dependencies as a political problem, which can be controlled by means defined normally as
political.  With his usual insight Marx anticipated both delusions
as epistemologically rooted in the opaque and recondite structure of
human dependency.  The relations of objective dependency:

 appear, in antithesis to those of personal dependency... in
 such a way that individuals are now ruled by abstractions,
 whereas earlier they depended on one another.... Relations
 can be expressed, of course, only in ideas, and thus philosophers have determined the reign of ideas to be the peculiarity of the new age, and have identified the creation
 of free individuality with the overthrow of this reign.  (9)

Neither type of social relations - either founded on personal or
impersonal dependence - can operate without goading human imagination
away from the genuine avenues of emancipation.  The system based on
personal dependence had to lean on the illusion of a supra-human,
extra-personal anchorage of the personal definition of status.  The
obverse is true of the system of impersonal dependence:  this is sustained and perpetuated by the illusion of personal freedom, the possibility of mastering, by an individual effort, the external relations
which constrain it.  It is precisely with the multitude's falling
under the spell of this illusion and behaving accordingly that the
web of impersonal dependencies is continually re-enacted and kept
alive.  The conditions of individual emancipation coincide with the
conditions that perpetuate the unfreedom of individuals 'en masse'.
A single individual, qua individual, may indeed 'get on top' of
social relations and subject them to his will;  so can a number of
individuals acting as an aggregate in a 'mechanical type' of solid-
arity.  But, by so doing, individuals all but strengthen the universal conditions of dependence and unfreedom.  This objective situation
sets individuals against one another; this is a situation in which
competition, the pursuit of individual interest to the detriment of
the interest of others, is the only rational and effective conduct.
More than that, the individual's treatment of other human beings as
an 'objective environment' which is to be mastered, is in itself an
expression of the fact that control over the individual's own fate
has been denied to him.  As Habermas aptly put it, 'those interests
which bind consciousness to the yoke imposed by the domination of
things and reified relations are, as material interests, anchored in
historically specific configurations of alienated labour, denied
satisfactions, and suppressed freedom'.  (10)

And thus any system of social interaction which presents the ends
and motives of such interaction as fixed and immutable (within the
framework of God's commandments, or the requirements of Reason) must
rely, for its perpetuation, on the authority of daily experience.
It is because the practical side of human experience is taken for
granted and unquestioned, and not seen in the relativizing, historical perspective, that the fundamental problems of individual freedom,
authenticity of life, fulfilment, etc., may be posited as epistemological questions alone, solvable by man perceived as an epistemological entity;  they may be seen, indeed, as part of a drama played
from beginning to end on the stage of intellect and meaning.  It is

not that such a view is oblivious to the intimate link between man's intellectual and practical life, between theory and social practice. On the contrary, the accumulated and intellectually processed evidence of social practice is seen as the proper foundation of infallibility of the solutions such view offers to the human quest for 'full life'.   The essential difference between such a view and critical sociology consists in the fact that the former considers the evidence of historically limited practice to be conclusive and, in actual fact, final, while the latter refuses to do so.   As Horkheimer emphatically declared in 1933, 'anthropology can offer no valid objection to the overcoming of bad social relations'.   (11) The only anthropology (aimed at being knowledge of universal human qualities) which is acceptable to critical sociology would be, in the words of Leo Kofler, a science 'of immutable premises of human mutability'.   One can take, as the founding principle of critical sociology, an a priori rejection of the possibility of invariant endowment – whether transcendental or natural – which characterizes the human species once and for all.   The only invariant attribute of the human species critical sociology will be prepared to accept is the mechanism by which the species becomes, ever anew and ever in a new form, the human species.   In 'German Ideology' Marx defined the production of new needs as the first historical act.   The production of new needs, which re-mould and re-classify the human environment, pushing to a new position the established borderline between the subjective and the objective, has always been, and will forever remain, the substance of human history.   The dividing line between what man can, and what he cannot be, may be clearly drawn only in reference to past practice;   but its extrapolation into the future will require an additional assumption, which critical sociology deems unsupportable – that the past contains evidence conclusively binding the future.

This assumption is built, however, into daily routine.   It is thanks to this assumption that commonsensical experience may supply reliable guidance to human behaviour.   Human organisms are endowed by nature with memory and the ability to learn, and such organisms can thrive only in an environment characterized by regularity and recurrent patterns of events.   Uncertainty arising from a sudden interruption of monotony is a source of terror:

> This is what is so frightening about a phenomenon like
> 'runaway inflation'.   In a money economy we experience
> the instability of currency in the social world much
> like we would an earthquake in the physical world.   When
> the foundations shake, anything can happen.   (12)

And thus human historical activity, as well as generating ever new needs and, consequently ever new forms of human relations, displays a tendency towards fixity and order.   It is true that this activity discloses previously unsuspected potentialities of man;   but the same activity leads to the elimination and suppression of other potentialities.   The essence of any order is in the augmentation of the probability of some occurrences and – by the same token – rendering other occurrences utterly improbable.   Critical sociology, having taken unlimited human potentiality as its organizing hypothesis, has to consider, as its major empirical concern, the way in which these potentialities come to be limited in actual social systems.

Commonsense and daily routine help and reinforce each other in sustaining and perpetuating both the fixed order of human inter- action and the universal belief that such fixity is ineluctable. Daily routine is structured in such a way that men are rarely, if ever, confronted with the fundamental choice between actual and potential forms of interaction, their life-process being split into the multitude of partial and seemingly inconsequential decisions. In fact, each successive link in the chain of their actions is to some extent limited by former actions - and the limitation grows pro- gressively in the course of individual biography, rendering the ques- tion of choice ever less realistic.   Commonsense, on the other hand, being a reflection of historically and biographically truncated ex- perience, confirms the universal validity of this individual lesson, and adds dignity to the necessity by drawing a sharp line between the 'rational' and 'reasonable' on the one hand, and 'irrational' and 'unrealistic' on the other.   For daily routine, commonsense is the major driving force.   For commonsense, daily routine is the ultimate source of cognitive certainty.   It is daily routine against which the truth of commonsensical, as well as of sociological, beliefs is measured.   Commonsense and daily routine being inextricably inter- twined, it does not matter much whether a sociology takes, as its object, daily routine (as Durksonian sociology does), or common- sense (as the existentialist critique of Durksonianism does);   in both cases sociology cuts the truth it seeks to the measure of his- torically restricted reality.   By the same token, consciously or un- wittingly, sociology falls in with that reality in its one-sided presentation of human potential.


CAN CRITICAL SOCIOLOGY BE A SCIENCE?

As we saw before, critical sociology tries to cut itself loose from both commonsense and daily routine as, respectively, its sources of information and the ultimate measure of truth.   This intention, in- dispensable if unfulfilled human potential is to be offered the status of a legitimate object of study, places in question, however, the scientific nature of the project.   In what sense may critical socio- logy claim a scientific status?   If critical sociology agrees that the only valid knowledge is true knowledge, what are its criteria of truth, once past experience and current daily routine have been denied this role?
   The concept of 'truth-process' is the response of critical socio- logy to this crucial objection.   The essential idea of truth as a historical process is contained in the following statement by Marx:
   The question whether human thinking can reach objective
   truth is not a question of theory but a practical question.
   In practice man must prove the truth, that is, actuality and
   power, this-sidedness of his thinking.   The dispute about
   the actuality or non-actuality of thinking - thinking isolated from practice - is a purely scholastic question.   (13)
In itself, however, this statement does not necessitate a decisive rupture from the positivist idea of truth.   Both Durksonian socio- logy and its existentialist critics would gladly agree that the supp- osition that men are indeed able to grasp objective truth will per-

haps never be conclusively verified, but that it does constitute a convenient working hypothesis which one is invited constantly to attempt to refute by putting it to a never-ending practical test. What is, after all, scientific inquiry in a most orthodox positivist sense, if not a series of practical tests of this hypothesis?   And yet, there is a wide and perhaps unbridgeable gap between the idea of truth contained in the quoted statement and the kind of truth positive sociology seeks for its statements.   This gap is not created, however, by the sheer linking of truth with the process of practical testing.   It is generated by a sharply different understanding of practice.

The practice to which positive sociology would refer its statements for testing and, possibly, for refutation is the practice of scientists - or the practice of an ordinary individual, but endowed, for the purpose at hand, with only such attributes as make him 'like' a scientist.   Such practice is distinguished by a sharp and immutable division of statuses between the person performing the testing and the object against which the testing is being performed.   It is a 'sine qua non' feature of this division that the testing agent only is aware of what is being tested.   This situation is normal in the case of the natural sciences.   In the social sciences, however, it must in most cases be artificially created - either by collecting data of objects' behaviour without their knowledge (as in most statistical studies), or by conveying to the objects deliberately incorrect information concerning the hypothesis about to be tested (as in most experiments in social psychology).   Thus an effort is made to ensure that the content of the hypothesis will not influence the process and the result of testing - i.e., the conduct of the objects of study.   Even though, in the case of social sciences, the objects of study are conscious human beings, endowed with the potential of knowing, understanding, and grasping meanings, they are deliberately placed, for the sake of the purity of procedure, in the position of objects which, like the objects of natural science, possess no such faculties.   Only then may the criteria of testing, as formulated by natural sciences, be applied to statements concerning the behaviour of human beings: an expectation is spelled out, a proper set of independent variables is selected or construed, and the ensuing conduct is compared with the initial expectations.   Significantly, the whole of the testing procedure consists of acts and events which remain entirely under the control of the scholar: throughout the procedure, he is the only 'knowing' agent; the only person aware of the specific meaning of events, assigned by the hypothesis under test.   The concept of testing, the meaning of verification or falsification - are all forged in such a way as to preserve the procedure as the exclusive domain of professional scholars or people reportedly copying their conduct.   One can almost define truth as statements supported by professional scientists.   Pragmatically, the activities of professional scientists are defined as truth-seeking and truth-finding; institutionally, scientists as a group are believed to ensure that persons attaining their approval will engage in such activities.   The concept of truth testing, which science supports, provides the foundation for the status of positive science as privileged, genuine knowledge.

If the rules of testing are applied to the study of human affairs,

scholars are obliged to eschew a meaningful dialogue with the objects
of their study.   Good research is expected to be thoroughly cleansed
of 'leading questions' - and certainly of any attempt at persuasion,
or changing objects' minds (unless proclivity to surrender to persuasion is itself the subject-matter of study), etc.   The social scientist would like to keep himself in the shadows as far as humanly
possible (the notorious one-way mirror of social psychologists being
an admirable embodiment of this tendency), and to make sure that his
physical presence - much more his presence as a meaning-establishing
agent - in no way 'distorts' the 'natural' course of events under
observation.   What he can find, therefore, and prove with the degree
of certainty allowed by the procedure, is how his objects would behave in routine conditions, assuming that their commonsensical definitions will retain their force.   Artifically, and with great care
and ingenuity, the human objects of sociological inquiry are kept or
placed in conditions in which they cannot, or would not, exercise
their faculties of understanding and decision-making, lest the 'validity' of inquiry be placed in danger.   Keeping men within the bounds
of their unfree daily existence is, therefore, built into the very
definition of legitimate scientific research and truth-testing.

As we have seen, the routine-commonsense compact has an in-built
tendency to self-perpetuation and assumes the appearance of its own
timelessness.   The routine-commonsense compact of the market society
is structured by the fundamental separation, within the life-process
of men, of the subjective ability to work, create, and authenticate
one's existence, and the objective conditions of such work, creativity, and authenticity.   Once split in such a way, the life-process
itself, 'in and by itself' posits the 'real objective conditions of
living labour' (material, instruments, etc.) 'as alien, independent
existences'.

> The objective conditions of living labour appear as separated,
> independent values opposite living labour capacity as sub-
> jective being .... Once this separation is given, the pro-
> duction process can only produce it anew, reproduce it, and
> reproduce it on an expanded scale.

The material on which living, subjective, labour works,

> is 'alien' material;   the instrument is likewise an 'alien' instru-
> ment;   its labour appears as mere accessory to their substance and
> hence objectifies itself in things not 'belonging to it'.

In this terse description of the essential structure of life-process
in a market society which separates objects of life labour from the
subjective, living source of the labour itself, we find both the
setting for routine activity and the epistemological roots of the
mode in which it is commonsensically experienced.   Routine and
associated commonsense form a vicious circle, which, unless cut at
some point, tends to reproduce itself 'on an expanded scale'.   A cut
capable of breaking the endless process of self-reproduction must be
an act of transcending merely commonsensical reflection, an act
stepping, though at the start only ideally, beyond commonsense:

> The recognition of the products as its own, and the judgement
> that its separation from the conditions of its realization
> is improper - forcibly imposed - is an enormous advance in
> awareness, itself the product of the mode of production
> resting on capital, and as much the knell to its doom as,

with the slave's awareness that he 'cannot be property of
another', with his consciousness of himself as a person,
the existence of slavery becomes a merely artificial,
vegetative existence, and ceases to be able to prevail as
the basis of production.  (14)

The death knell to the allegedly invulnerable routine-commonsense
compact sounds when the habitual split is suddenly seen in the light
of another possibility.   Then, and only then, does the natural begin
to be perceived as artificial, the habitual as enforced, the normal
as unbearable.   Once the harmony between the routine condition and
commonsensical knowledge has been distorted, the whole network of
social relations is set in motion, and the iron laws of 'normal'
behaviour are put in abeyance.   The allegedly invariant attributes
of men and their social life reveal their historicity.

The interests of emancipation and the interests of technical mastery served by positive science seem to be, therefore, at cross purposes.   Science, as we have seen, lacks the means of breaking the
routine commonsense compact and, moreover, refuses to acquire it,
pointing to its impeccable truth-testing rules as on insuperable objection.   Such rules require that science may investigate only those
objects which remain wholly under the scientists' cognitive control;
science continues to supply reliable knowledge, that is, conclusive
information it can vouch for, only in so far as those men whose conduct it describes remain objects, i.e., thing-like, due to the un-
broken hold of the habit-enforcing routine conditions of life, over
which they have no control.   Emancipation starts, however, when
those conditions cease to be seen 'as they really are', when they
are postulated in a form which, for being not-yet-real, eludes scientific methodology and the test of truth.   The question arises,
therefore, that perhaps the apparent gap between positive science
and emancipatory knowledge is indeed unbridgeable as it seems at
first sight, and as extremists and purists on both sides insist.
The question is crucial to both social science and the prospects of
human emancipation.   If the gap is really unbridgeable, the social
sciences may well be condemned to the role of one of the agents
recording or even fortifying the already accomplished split of men
into subjects and objects of action, while interests in emancipation
may be doomed to rambling over uncharted, slushy ground of uncontrolled fantasy.   The answer hinges, it seems, on the possibility of a
re-adjustment of science's concept of truth-testing.

No wonder that in recent years a number of attempts have been
made to blaze trails which may bring the vehicle of science beyond
the spell-bound circle of routine and commonsense.   The common
motive of all these attempts has been the search for reliable, testable, conclusive knowledge of phenomena unlike those reliably explored by positive social science: namely, the non-routinized, still
irregular, out-of-the-ordinary phenomena, observable or just conceivable, which, in a sense, can be considered as a glimpse into the
future, or into an alternative reality.   We will now briefly discuss several such attempts.

Appalled by the spectacular bankruptcy of French academic sociology, which failed to forecast the outburst of student rebellion
and class conflict inside that allegedly pacified and consensus-
bound country, Edgar Morin came forward in 1968 with the idea of a

'sociology of the present', (15) as an alternative to sociology traditionally centred upon timeless regularity (i.e., regularity described without reference to variables which represent qualitatively
changeable time).   Not unexpectedly, the central unit of the alternative sociology was to represent, (in opposition to 'action' or
'role', the basic units of traditional sociological analysis) the intention to grasp the irregular and the unique.   And this central
unit, in Morin's view, was the event - 'l'événement, qui signifie
l'irruption à la fois du vécu, de l'accident, de l'irréversibilité,
du singulier concret dans le tissu de la vie sociale', and which, for
the same reason, 'est le monstre de la sociologie'.   Derided and
shunned by academic sociology, the event, however, displays a number
of attributes which make it ideally suitable for the role of a vantage point from which the realm of the possible can be scanned.

> The event, from the sociological point of view, is anything
> which cannot be squeezed into statistical regularities.
> Hence a crime or a suicide are not events, in so far as they
> may be inscribed into some statistical regularity, while a
> 'wave' of criminality, or epidemy of suicide can be con-
> sidered as events, alongside the death of president Kennedy
> or suicide of Marilyn Monroe.

The event is 'news';   it contains information, inasmuch as information is the part of the message which conveys novelty.   The event
is, therefore, by definition, a de-structuring factor. By its very
presence - or, rather, by the fact of being perceived as an event -
it perturbs the systems of rationalization, which enforce intelligibility upon the relation between the spirit and its everyday world.
The event questions this intelligibility, and by so doing inspires
critical scepticism towards rationalizing illusions.   Instead, it
puts on the agenda the need for a theory which selects as its foundation extreme situations, paroxysms of history, 'pathological' phenomena rather than statistical uniformities.

Crisis is precisely such an event.   Thanks to the unusual con-
centration of out-of-the-ordinary features, the inherent instability
which defies orderly, deterministic description, and its extreme
evolutionary flexibility, the crisis acts as a sudden revelation of
'latent, subterranean realities' which remain invisible in times
defined as 'normal'.   Following Marxian-Freudian strategy, one can
view the crisis as the unique occasion of seeing through the veil of
the routine, directly into the 'genuine', or at least the genuinely
important, reality - that which is submerged, unconscious or infra-
structural.   Such a view of the crisis will, of course, jarringly
differ from the treatment offered by academic sociology with its
apprehensive dismissal of crisis as an event which is both marginal
and epiphenomenal:   a case of momentary technical failure of the
social fabric, which cannot be dressed in the vocabulary employed to
express the main subject-matter of social science.   'Finalement la
crise unit en elle, de façon trouble et troublante, répulsive et
attractive, le caractère accidentel (contingent, événementiel), le
caractère de nécessité (par la mise en oeuvre des réalités les plus
profondes, les moins conscientes, les plus déterminantes) et le
caractère conflictuel'.   The clinching argument in favour of the
crisis as the true object of sociological analysis, is, therefore,
that the crisis is a richer source of information than ordinary life,

on which sociologists have focussed their attention.   Granted that
positive science is set upon the true and precise description of
'reality over there', here is an opening which permits the fulfilment
of this task better than other occasions, since, through it, can be
discerned parts of reality otherwise hermetically sealed off.   What
Morin in fact suggests is an extension of sociological strategy and
method to those vast expanses so far laid fallow, but promising to
bring in an unusually rich harvest.   Morin is making a plea on behalf of a new object of exploration, thus far either neglected or unduly underrated.

Morin hopes that this new object of research, thanks to its unique
features, will have a feedback effect on the status of the sociologist in the course of his research.   In this important respect Morin
steps beyond the modest reform already proposed by Coser and other
American Simmelians, who, having suggested that conflict rather than
consensus should be the proper object of sociological inquiry, have
proceeded to analyse this new object in traditional, functionalist
terms.   Morin thinks that the crisis, conceived as a spontaneous,
self-developing process rather than another 'functional pre-requisite'
of a rigid system, will force the student into permanent self-
criticism.   This will be a considerable improvement on academic
sociology in its entirety, where 'la prétention ridicule du "marxiste-
léniniste" althussérien à monopoliser la science et à rejeter comme
idéologie ce qui est hors de la doctrine n'a d'égale que celle du
grand manager en sondages, qui rejette comme idéologie tout ce qui
introduit le doute et la critique dans la sociologie officielle'.
Self-criticism, the permanent revision of students' views, the realization that no set of research techniques can be trusted with the
job of sifting the nugget of truth from the dross of appearances,
will secure the proper dialectic relationship between the observer
and the observed phenomenon.   Morin is so overwhelmed by the dazzling prospects of crisis analysis, that he does not hesitate to describe the role played by the sociologist as an actor in the events
under scrutiny.   He exemplifies his forecast by invoking the Nan-
terre experience of half-baked would-be sociologists sweeping away
the over-cooked dish of stale academic truisms.

It is, however, a very limited concept of actor which sustains
Morin's far-fetched hopes.   Having been transformed into actor, in
a somewhat facile manner, by the sheer fact of being sceptical, the
sociologist still remains a purely epistemological being, much like
his more traditional predecessors.   His only gain is his own self-
criticism (an improvement, to be sure, not to be lightly dismissed);
he still stays enclosed in the universe of pure meanings;   the in-
toxicating feeling of changing the world turns out, under closer
scrutiny, to come from changing the world of his ideas only.   His
praxis is cut to the measure of academic theory;   his dialogue is
among equals, a debate among students of reality rather than with
reality itself.   Morin's recipe is for the emancipation of the
sociologist from the blinkers of commonsense:   something to be
strongly desired - but as a preliminary step, rather than as a
finished emancipating alternative to sociology.   There is, however,
no further step in Morin's itinerary.   He leaves us to hope for the
joyful liberation of sociologists' imagination.   Yet we do not know
how the precious liberty of scholars will link - if at all - with the

prospect of the emancipation of man.   In short, Morin's is an offer
to perform somewhat better, with more insight and perceptiveness,
what is essentially the traditional role of positive sociology, confronting the human world as an object 'over there', which can be
described, but not communicated with.

As we shall now see, yet another attempt to break through the
fetters of commonsensical recanting of reality – made by Henry S.
Kariel in 1969 (16) – stops short of an open challenge to the strategy of positive sociology.   Lacking the rejuvenating experience
of the Paris spring, and perhaps put off as much as stimulated by
the wilder aspects of social unrest in the 1960s, Kariel is even
more careful than Morin in circumscribing his programme as one for
'professional use' only.   Like Morin, he locates the remedy in the
field of object-selection and the choice of analytical framework.
Differences in wording conceal the structural identity of programmes.
If Morin dubs his ideal for social science as a sociology of the
present, Kariel, on the other hand, singles out the preoccupation
with the present as the undoing of academic sociology.   'The constitution of the present, they assume, is valid, or at least given.
For them, "the present" is not so much a concept as a benign state
of being'.   The original sin of positive social science consists
precisely in its inability, or unwillingness, to lift itself above
the horizon of the present.   Even the practitioners of futuristics,
who claim the mantle of utopians – made only of the most solid and
reliable modern fibre:

> begin with the present, that which 'is'.   They perceive
> what various forms of system analysis have shown to exist:
> man as egotistical utility and power maximizer, public
> policy as interest groups inputs, the economic sector as
> primary generator of community goods, governmental
> structures as hierarchical organizations, politics as a
> sacrifice of personal values, psychological and economic
> resources as scarce, and development as whatever leads
> toward the fulfillment of this empirically confirmed
> vision.

The trouble is, however, that the present itself is a complex product of past battles, and therefore starting from the present as a
trustworthy baseline – objective and just as reasonable as we have
been made to believe – means in fact 'to acquiesce in the policies
of those in society who have the power to create reality, who are
free enough to structure man's consciousness of space and time'.
Such 'acquiescence' follows from presenting the unreal as the impossible;   and presenting it as such is a necessary consequence of
the decision to serve technical-instrumental interests, and consequently to advance positive science, which cannot be achieved otherwise.

Now what about the alternative?   Like Morin, Kariel conceives of
it as an intellectual operation.   He would, given a chance, probably quote with approval Lyman and Scott's declaration of the
principles of their 'sociology of the absurd':

> One can study the social world from the point of view of
> the superior or the subordinate;   of the lover or his
> mistress;   of the bourgeoisie or the proletariat;   of
> management or labour;   of the deviant or the person who

labels him deviant;  and so on.   What is important is
that one should have a perspective, but the particular perspective employed is irrelevant to the rectitude of theorizing.   One can make true statements from any perspective,
including those not consonant with any available ideology.   (17)
The problem of truth is easy because there are many truths, no one
better than the other, and each one remaining truthful only within
the framework of an ideology.   The inequality of ideologies in their
practice of fixing social reality, in their access to the change of
sedimenting objective structures, is to be offset the easy way - by
proclaiming their intellectual equality.   And then the sociologist
is able sedulously to conform to positive criteria of truth-testing
('rectitude of theorizing') while disregarding the constraints imposed on truth-selection by the routine-commonsense compact, in the
shaping of which various ideologies (existing and conceivable) play
a highly unequal role.
   Similarly, Kariel invites us to consider politics, or indeed
social life, as a play, in which there are players, each with his
own characteristic vantage point;  none can be legitimately selected,
on intellectual grounds alone, as privileged, more 'truthful' than
the rest.

   To perceive this expressive aspect of experience, we need
   merely follow the clues of Hannah Arendt and conceptualize
   political action as a form of play, as characteristically a
   performing act....  Should we wish to understand the way
   action signifies the presence of ordinarily unrealized
   structures of being, we cannot regard it as conclusively
   significant in any other sense, for example, of 'really'
   signifying some predefined intention or of being 'really'
   functional to some predefined structure.   We must see it
   as a form of play:  complete in itself.

Kariel seems to dispose of the troublesome question of testing the
truth of statements which challenge commonsensical 'hard facts'
simply by denying, by the power of words alone, the presence of such
facts.   There are no 'predefined structures' which channel the
course of the game independently of players' realized or unrealized
needs;  there are no 'predefined intentions' which are forcibly
attached to the positions from which individual players start their
game.   The play is 'complete in itself', so let us stop worrying
about how to detach it from the strings of inert routine:  it is not
attached to them to start with.   It is only misled and misleading
social science which has encouraged us to believe as much.   What we
need in order to endow our products with emancipatory power, is simply to shift our 'attention à la vie' toward new regions, and sym-
pathetically look through the cognitive perspectives of all partners.
'Valuing the needs of the child over those of the existing school,
or ...the needs of the worker over those of the organization, they
(sociologists following this advice - Z.B.) introduce options.
Positing countervailing values, they enlarge understanding'.   Again,
as in Morin, the rest is silence:  we do not know how such 'enlarged
understanding' gained by sociologists or political scientists may
possibly result in an extension of the freedom of men.   In effect,
it is only the sociologist who is likely to gain in his own, intellectual, emancipation, by visiting diverse observation points, since

the players themselves have been already entrenched, perhaps too
well, in observation points of their own.    Kariel, like Morin,
seems to be preoccupied, perhaps unwittingly, with the unbinding of
the sociologists' imagination rather than of the men they imagine.
All truths are relative, partial and one-sided;  everybody knows his
partial truth anyway;  let sociologists, therefore, enjoy insight
into all truths, instead of falling into the conservative trap of
futilely pursuing the only, real, genuine truth.    What sets sociologists apart and here defines their unique professional role is not
truth-testing, but ironic distance from truths:  sociologists alone
know, what others are too blinkered to notice, that truths are many
and all are faulty.    Here lies the crucial difference between Kariel
and Morin.    The first denies the existence of this 'depth' of reality
which the latter would wish us to penetrate.    Explicitly, Kariel
proposes to analyse social life as a play.    In actual fact, his programme boils down to an invitation to an intellectual play, extended
to sociologists alone.

Manfred Stanley (18) likewise considers the question of the way in
which social science may transcend commonsense, but posits it somewhat differently, refusing to budge from the position that truth -
one and indivisible - can in principle be established, that establishing it is a worthy occupation, and that this occupation is the
domain of science.    He is, however, aware, that the commonsensically
'obvious', and empirically most clearly given reality, is not the only
frame within which truth can be measured.    If there are other
frames, they must nevertheless be empirically accessible, even if in
a much more tedious and intricate way.    Stanley wishes to show that
one can, while proceeding according to the rules of empirically
founded positive science, still render the scholarly discussion of
potential realities legitimate and valid.

The hope Morin attached to the phenomenon of crisis, Stanley
links, more specifically, to the process of 'delegitimation'.
Stanley agrees with the ruling Durksonian paradigm in that the
'normalcy' of a social order is founded on successful legitimation,
i.e., wide acceptance of norms, values, and meanings which uphold the
kind of behaviour which ultimately enacts and re-enacts the web of
relationships perceived as the order in question.    Hence 'delegitimation' stands for any disruption of the order - all cases in which
significant pockets of population, or sections of publicly relevant
behaviour are deflected from the routine pattern of conduct.    On
the strength of the tacitly accepted paradigm, unusual behaviour is
to be linked, for the sake of explanation, to some set of mental
processes.    Stanley calls such processes 'experienced deprivation'.
Contrary to the habitual view of the majority of sociologists, delegitimation is not an episodic event, a departure from the 'natural
state', caused by moral unintelligibility, ignorance, or psychologically prompted deviance.    It is, on the contrary, a constant and,
in its own way, regular phenomenon, which provides a willing sociologist with the permanent opportunity of catching a glimpse of
reality cleansed of one-sided commonsensical interpretations.    It is
constant because the experience of deprivation results from scarcity,
which in its turn is a permanent feature of the social order.    We
know since Durkheim's times at least, that any society goes so far in
inspiring respect and desire for its values that sooner or later it

finds it difficult to deliver on its own pledge:   there are normally
more people attracted by society-supported values, than values to be
offered, distributed and appropriated.   One can almost say that de-
sirability and scarcity of values are inextricably linked to each
other.   Hence, scarcity is a 'normal' phenomenon - and given the
normalcy of scarcity, one may expect the experience of deprivation
to be fairly common.   Finally, people who experience their situation as deprivation will sooner or later be prompted to act in such
a way as to minimize that unpleasant experience, and a change of
social order will take place as a result.

Thus far we are still well within the habitual universe of discourse of mainstream academic sociology.   Stanley's is, therefore,
an interesting attempt to develop a strategy of testing knowledge
about alternative, non-routine realities, by means which are considered legitimate by Durksonian social knowledge, and may be accommodated to the dominant paradigm.   Essentially, Stanley's strategy
consists in what one might call 'mental experimenting', which, however, at no point, departs from empirically accessible features of
present or past reality.   It is by carefully exploring the present
reality and scanning the logic of past occurrences, that one can establish sound answers to the following questions:

First, in what specific ways can a given society (viewed
as a structure of meanings) be thought of as a field of
'potential scarcities'?   Second, under what conditions
are such potentialities selectively concretized into
'experienced patterns of deprivation' among particular
sectors of the population?   Third, under what conditions
are these experiential deprivations linked to remedial
social action?

Stanley, as we see, assumes the regularity of 'irregular' behaviour;
starting from this assumption, one can as safely predict disruption
of the current order as one does, encouraged or absolved by the
Durksonian paradigm (and, for good measure, by its critics), predict its continuity and perpetuation.   Hence, in principle, one can
empirically investigate, and predict on empirical grounds, the conditions under which such disruption of the present order may take
place, which will eventually lead to the emancipation of man - to the
establishment of human freedom.

Emancipation, as one might expect, is also defined in terms of
meanings.   Freedom:

means that every person is an interpreter of the meanings
that comprise the social world, i.e. a hermeneutical
agent.   Indeed, social control essentially is the particular socio-cultural process through which the fact of
every person's moral agency is successfully concealed from
particular categories of the population and differentially
delegated to other sectors.

Lack of freedom, in other words, results from a part of society being
deprived of, or surrendering, or not realizing, their meaning-,
purpose- and norm-establishing faculty, and relying in these vital
respects on the discretion of others.   Similarly, power in society
consists in monopoly or privilege in the field of meaning-interpret-
ation and lasts as long as the latter continues.   Stanley senses in
the phenomenon of power so defined the permanent source of ever re-

curring experiences of deprivation.   Power, so to speak, generates
resistance to itself which in turn leads towards its progressive
limitation.   This progress is entirely located in the sphere of
meanings;  liberation is a matter of illumination, and hence, almost
by definition, co-extensive with the activity of social science.
The intimate relation between emancipation and the social sciences is
assured by the nature of the first.   Now that we have satisfied ourselves that social science can deal with alternative realities without violating its own rules of truth-testing, we can see how a revolution in society can be tackled by sociological means without revo-
lutionizing sociology itself.

Stanley's sociologist is again an observer and a detached analyst.
It is true that his interest is in alternative realities rather than
in the accomplished one.   But whatever his cognitive objectives, the
present - the only field accessible to empirical investigation -
remains the sole object of his research.   In fact, Stanley proposes
to apply the principles sociologists always jealously guarded, to
problems they did not dare to attack:  if sociologists, traditionally,
restrict themselves to sorting out the real and the realistic from
among the interpretations of current reality, Stanley wishes to
stretch the field of such sorting to embrace possible realities,
still located in the future.   If Stanley were right, then the sociologist could, in advance, on the strength of available and testable
evidence, sort out the 'true', realistic extrapolations of the
present, from a pool of possibilities albeit much larger than any
ordinary sociologist would at present be prepared to consider.   The
extrapolations Stanley explores include those which - far from assuming a smooth continuation of present trends - presage a drastic reversal of the current routine and commonsensical meaning interpretations.   With eyes properly aimed and focussed, one can discern, in
the universe of facts ordinarily covered by research, signs of emerging scarcity (a lack of community, which finds its expression in
increasingly fashionable nostalgia - the 'perception of the past in
terms of the phenomenology of present scarcities' - being a characteristic example);  knowing, in addition, again from testable evidence,
the condition under which such scarcity is likely to engender the
experience of deprivation, and when such experience may lead to a
remedial action, one can sort out, in a way legitimized by positive
science, the truth of a prediction apparently at odds with the realities of to-day.   What Stanley leaves unsaid is the major irritant
of all seekers of true knowledge about the future:  the feedback
effect of the prediction.   Its presence will inevitably trigger off
some action, which will make the content of prediction more or less
probable - more or less 'true':  the prediction will be 'fed' into
reality, and, subsequently, reality will be different from what it
was before.   Stanley, in line with the general tendency of positive
sociology, does his best to enclose the totality of the testing process, complete with its conclusive and irreversible findings, within
the area directly controlled - and, indeed, structured - by the tester
himself;   thereby preserving the exclusive rights of the sociological
profession to validate men's knowledge of their affairs, only now
also including men's future.

We have considered thus far three, fairly typical, proposals of
the solution to the vexing dilemma of transcending commonsense while

retaining the possibility of testing the truth of alternative interpretations.   None of the three seems entirely satisfactory.   Apart
from their essential similarities, each points in a somewhat different direction, each being prepared to sacrifice another parcel of
the institutionalized habits of positive social science.   Kariel's
sacrifice seems to be the most radical of the three;  but then it
goes beyond acceptable limits, in fact begging the question by disavowing the very concept of truth testing and, indeed, of truth as
such.   Having done that he can offer us little help in our search.
For a similar reason, we can draw little inspiration from another
radical solution, proposed half a century ago by Ernst Bloch in the
recently increasingly popular 'Geist der Utopie'.   Bloch assumes
from the start the ahistorical, truly anthropological nature of
'Prinzip Hoffnung' — the genuine springboard of the perpetual quest
for human emancipation.   The thrust for emancipation, as well as
such progress as has actually been made in history, is ascribed to
an elusive faculty of the drive toward 'regnum humanum', toward yet-
unfulfilled perfection — a genuine 'telos' built into human kind,
more lasting than human history and more powerful than any historically erected barriers to human self-perfection.   If that were so,
then concrete investigations of specific historic conditions can do
little in illuminating the human potential of generating alternative
realities.   The drive towards the Kingdom of Reason is in itself
irrational and cannot be presented as an orderly, deterministic, or
indeed regular process.   Much like Munchhausen by his hair, man can
lift himself above his historical condition simply by a sudden recognition of what authentic being could be.   Man's essence is always in front of him, pursued but not caught up with, to be found
only deep in man's hopes, but not in anything already crystallized
in his existence.

> The real nature of the essence is not something already
> found in a finished form, like water, air, or fire, or
> even an invisible universal idea, or whatever figure may
> be used to absolutize or hypostatize these real quanta.
> The real or the essence is that which does not yet exist,
> which is in quest of itself in the core of things, and
> which is awaiting its genesis in the trend latency of the
> process .... Of course, the Not-Yet must not be thought of
> as though there already existed, say in the atom or in the
> subatomic 'differentials' of matter, everything that would
> later emerge, already present and encapsulated in minuscule
> form as inherent disposition.  (19)

There is nothing, therefore, in the sensually accessible, accomplished reality, which can throw light on the vast expanse of the unfulfilled human potential.   In choosing the vantage point for the
critique of reality we can count on the guidance of nothing more
reliable and trustworthy than our capability of postulating the
vantage point we have chosen.   It is conscience, in which 'the still
distant totality is reflected', and philosophy which 'opens ultimately at and in the horizon of the future', which constitute the true
'point of Archimedes', lending human action enough support to turn
the course of history upside down.  (20) Bloch's is truly an En-
lightenment-like call for courage and self-reliance:  knowing is
daring, the search for knowledge and the search for certainty go

different ways, for, in order to advance on the road to truly emancipating knowledge, man closes his eyes to things posited by the
reality-at-hand as certainties.   Nowhere has man's hope been conclusively victorious, but it has not been ultimately frustrated
either.   Men will go on hoping whatever happens, since hoping for
the not-yet-reached essence is the truly human existence.

Potentiality, alternative, future, hope - all these are to Bloch
descriptive categories of human reality, and not methodological precepts for sociology.   His interest in emancipation stems from the
same preoccupation as Heidegger's interest in hermeneutics.   It is
elucidation of human existence rather than the construction of an objective science of this existence, which Bloch, like Gadamer, is
after.   And a sociologist searching for hard-and-fast methodological
rules for an 'emancipatory science' is bound to be as frustrated
reading Bloch, as a historian in search of cut-and-dried rules of
'understanding history' will be studying Heidegger.

All the other ideas considered thus far, do intend to offer a
practical counsel to sociologists.   In order to do so, they all agree
that the verification of emancipatory knowledge, if at all conceivable, is the business of social scientists;  to be admitted as attainable, it must be construed in such a way that it may be accomplished, in all its stages, by and inside the community of the students
of human affairs (sociologists or philosophers).   For all the
authors we have discussed above, as well as for their more orthodox
colleagues, the genuine meaning of the question 'how can knowledge of
alternative realities be tested?' boils down, though often implicitly,
to the question 'how can knowledge of alternative realities be conclusively tested by scientists and by means only they employ?'   It
is back to this common, though tacit, assumption, that the failure to
reach a satisfactory solution can be traced.   There is one sacrifice
not one single author we have so far visited has been prepared to
accept:  the sacrifice of the unique, privileged vantage point of
social scientists and their self-sufficiency as the judges of the
true and the untrue.

This last, but decisive, step has been made by Jurgen Habermas -
perhaps by Habermas alone - in his recent re-interpretation of the
Marxian view of the relation between social knowledge and social
reality.   Articulating the Gramscian tradition of Marxism in the
vernacular of modern social science, Habermas stands the chance of
getting the message through to that audience which has viewed with
equanimity offers wrapped in unfamiliar vocabulary.   In direct discourse with modern sociology and its most topical problems, Habermas
re-states the Marxian case for truth-process - for the course of
truth-verification to be extended beyond the laboratory field ad-
ministered by professional scientists, and so to be transformed into
the process of authentication.


TRUTH AND AUTHENTICATION

There are three interests, which, according to Habermas, generate
human preoccupation with knowledge and crystallize in theoretical
statements about facts, and in cognitive strategies.   These are
technical, practical, and emancipatory interests.   The first two,

though aimed at different aspects of practice, share a common status. From 'communication' - the pre-reflective articulation of routine practice, the commonsensical recognition of 'facts' - they detach 'discourse', free from the immediate compulsions of action, which is subject to its own, reasoned rules and is able to supply reasoned justification of what has been simply recognized as factual.   It is thanks to the relative autonomy of discourse that theoretical state-ments about the phenomenal domain of things and events (in the case of the technical interest), or persons and utterances (in the case of the practical interest) can be made and justified.   The autonomy of discourse is never complete.   It is always set in motion by the ne-cessities or queries arising from within the practice of communicat-ion;   and its results, if they be of practical application, are ex-pected to be fed back into the mainstream of rationally orientated action and orientations of everyday communication.   But the process of the justification of theoretical statements, of the transformation of the 'merely recognized' into 'actually known', is wholly enclosed in the realm of discourse, where it can be consciously and purpose-fully controlled and rule-regulated.   In so far as communication may be seen as an anthropological, generic condition of man, so technical and practical interests  arise immediately from all communication, as unavoidable attempts 'to clarify the "constitution" of the facts about which theoretical statements are possible'.   (21)  Being governed by its own set of rules, which - unlike the stuff they are applied to and the products of their application - are in no way embedded in, or dependent on, that communication which constitutes the texture of social life, discourse can legitimately claim a transcendental status, which is subsequently upheld and embodied in the autonomy of its holders (the scientists) as the knowing agents and the testers of valid theory.

The status of emancipatory interest, and the kind of knowledge which may result from its exertion, however, is different.   Above all, emancipatory interest - contrary to Bloch - is not an extra-temporal, generic feature of the condition of man as a communicating being.   'This interest can only develop to the degree to which re-pressive force, in the form of the normative exercise of power, pre-sents itself permanently in structures of distorted communication - that is, to the extent that domination is institutionalized'.   Dis-torted communication constitutes a situation of inequality between the partners of a dialogue;   a situation in which one of the partners is incapable, or incapacitated, to the extent of not being able to take up a symmetrical posture toward his opposite number, to per-ceive and to assume the other roles operative in the dialogue.   Such a situation is effected, on a permanent basis (if measured by the life-span of men involved), by institutionalized domination, which deprives some partners from those means and assets without which taking an equal stand in dialogue becomes impossible.   Only then can emancipatory interest emerge:   it is, from the outset, a product of social and/or individual history.

Emancipatory interest is, therefore, interest in elucidating this history.   It prompts the actor to bring up, to the level of consc-iousness (where they can be critically mastered), the unseen occurr-ences and actions which have shaped the present situation and sus-tain it as distorted communication.   In so doing, the actor is helped by the 'rational reconstruction' of rule systems, which scientific discourse makes explicit and which determines the way in which experience can be processed and justified.   But the dialogue which serves the emancipatory interest is not in itself such discourse. Nor does it aim to be the justification of the validity of the experiential recognition of 'facts'.   Unlike discourse which arises from technical and practical interest, the dialogue actuated by emancipatory interest cannot be, at any stage, detached from its practical engagement in communication, in the life-process.   It does not confine itself to the objective of reasoned justification;  it wants, in addition, to test itself in the actual acceptance of its hypothetical solution in the praxis of the partners.   It seeks not only to validate itself, but to 'authenticate'.   It involves, therefore, a different, wider notion of truth-testing.   The hypotheses it brings to light are vindicated when the partner in the dialogue accepts and takes up the role of which he has been deprived in the course of distorted communication.   In Habermas's view, psychoanalytic therapy provides a typical pattern for the dialogue activated by emancipatory interest.

> In the patient's acceptance of the 'worked out' interpretations which the doctor suggests to him and his confirming that these are applicable, he at the same time sees through a self-deception.   The true interpretation at the same time makes possible the authentic intention of the subject with respect to these utterances, with which he has till then deceived himself (and possibly others).   Claims to authenticity as a rule can only be tested within the context of action.   That distinctive communication in which the distortions of the communicative structure themselves can be overcome is the only one in which claims to truth can be tested 'discursively' together and simultaneously with a claim to authenticity, or be rejected as unjustified .

By its very constitution, the critical knowledge serving emancipatory interest differs from remaining types of knowledge in the way it is tested: it cannot be vindicated within the framework of institutionalized discourse, a domain of the experts.   In the process of its vindication the experts - the institutionalized holders of tested knowledge which makes the 'rational reconstruction' of facts plausible - play an active, perhaps a crucial, role;  but they do not monopolistically control the process.   Nor may their verdict, argued solely in terms of discourse proper, be considered as final and conclusive, unless 'authenticated', i.e. confirmed in the act of rectification of communicative distortions.   This realization sets Habermas apart from all previously considered sociologists who offered solutions to the problem of tested critical knowledge. They all, as we remember, tried to squeeze the problem of testing within the inadequate framework of institutionalized, scientist-operated, 'discourse'.   They neglected the distinctive feature of 'dialogue' in which emancipatory hypotheses need to be vindicated. They neglected as well the paramount difference between 'reasoned justification', which is the end-ideal of discourse, and 'authentication', which is the requisite of dialogue.

   Discourse - the mode of existence of positive science, which illuminates the constitution of reality in response to technical and practical interests - provides only the first, preliminary stage of the emancipatory process which reaches into realms positive science resolutely, and justifiably, refuses to trespass.   It is by the positive analysis of reality, which seeks its legitimation in the sedulous application of the ordinary fact-finding means of positive social science, that the hypotheses of critical knowledge, aimed at the restitution of undistorted communication, are first advanced. At this stage, their truth or untruth is testable in a way which is in no respect different from other statements participating in the discourse.   Since, however, what they propose is precisely the un-fitness of the current condition to make the hypotheses workable, the impossibility of revealing their truth in the present situation of distorted communication, then the conditions of 'normal' commu-nication (i.e., founded on the equality of partners) must first be established to lend the required authority to the results of the test.   Critical knowledge asserts that current reality has the character of distorted communication.   This assertion can be vindi-cated only if the communication comes to be mended.   This, however, requires, in turn, the removal of the institutionalized dominance responsible for the distortions.   In other words, it requires organ-ized action.   Authentication - becoming-true-in-the-process - can occur only in the realm of praxis, of which the institutionalized, partial discourse of professional scientists constitutes only the initial stage.   And so, the crucial question of authentication (in opposition to verification) is:   'How can the translation of theory into praxis be appropriately organized?'   (22)

In the case of psychoanalytic dialogue, this translation is made relatively simple by the willing submission of the patient.   Though the process is by no means free of friction and, time and again, there are violent conflicts, the willingness on the part of one of the partners to conform to the role of patient helps the dialogue round most awkward corners.   This assumption by no means holds in social life.   Both the proponents of critical knowledge, and its possible recipients, may agree (though not inevitably) to the dis-tribution of doctor and patient roles.   The advocates of critique may refuse to attempt to enter meaningful dialogue with some of their potential partners and assume their inability to maintain such a dia-logue.   The possible recipients of critical knowledge may refuse to consider themselves as patients, and instead will view all attempts at re-defining reality as threats aimed at the very foundation of their routine existence which they do not experience as unfreedom. In case the critical hypothesis fails, by design or by default, to guide the partner's reflection and thereby to 'dissolve barriers to communication', it is forced to remain on the level of discourse and to forbear the chance of being transformed into a dialogue.   It becomes then indistinguishable from other theoretical statements, and, like them, may be tested only as other statements are:   as an expectation, whose content is compared with the actual development of processes in which the statement in question is not an operating factor.   Hypotheses like Marx's prediction of the future trends of capitalist accumulation become statements testable by the ordinary means of positive science, in so far as they remain on the level of institutionalized discourse;   posit the groups, whose situation is shaped by the above trends, as objects outside the discourse;   and

refuse, or are barred from, entering into some meaningful dialogue
with such groups with the intention of influencing their processes of
self-reflection.   It is not the values chosen, or a peculiar critical scepticism, which sets off emancipatory knowledge as a body of
statements qualitatively distinct from technical or practical knowledge.   The genuine, and only, distinction is located on the verifi-
cation-authentication axis;   in other words, in the relation practically entered into by the knowledge in question with daily routine
and its commonsensical reflection.   In so far as this routine, complete with commonsense, remains in the position of a nature-like
object 'outside' the realm of discourse (in such a way that its attributes are untouched by the fact that, within that discourse,
certain hypotheses have been formulated) there is no reason to classify such hypotheses separately, as belonging to a special type of
knowledge, serving other than technical and/or practical interests.
This is a very important point, only too often misunderstood by scholars imprisoned within the arid 'fact-value' dilemma.   Knowledge
does not become critical or emancipatory by manifesting its dislike
of reality or attaching a string of invectives to statements of fact.
Nor can a statement claim emancipatory potential if it does not diligently observe the facts, retaining its impeccability as a factual
statement.   Within the framework of institutionalized scientific
discourse, there is no evident difference in content, or in syntax,
between statements which will eventually remain inside the cycle of
technical and practical interests and their fulfilment, and those
statements which may potentially address themselves to emancipatory
interest.   Such difference is brought into relief only beyond the
framework of institutionalized discourse proper - when some statements, unlike others, start interacting with the actors they describe, transplanting routine life and its commonsensical reflection
from the 'outside' into the 'inside' of communication, and passing
from professional discourse into an open dialogue.

The emancipatory potential of knowledge is put to the test - and,
indeed, may be actualized - only with the beginning of dialogue, when
the 'objects' of theoretical statements turn into active partners in
the incipient process of authentication.   This type of relationship
was exemplified by Marx as the interaction between social science -
the scientific theory of capitalism - and the working class.   Marx
guessed that there was nothing in the objective predicament of
workers which could protect communication barriers against the erod-
ing impact of true social theory.   Unlike the bourgeoisie, they
would not consider an alternative reality, cleansed of the current
form of dominance, to be a direct threat to the conditions which constitute the only acceptable, conceivable social identity.   This is
why exposure of the historical roots of dominance and the objective
determinants of distorted communication, stood a chance of being
willingly received by the workers, assigned to the losing end of the
distortion.   On this ground Marx expected the workers to take up,
willingly and enthusiastically, the role of 'patients', in order to
bring the causes of their condition to light, to re-define them and
then to re-make them in the course of rationally conceived practical
action.

In general terms, the genuine confirmation of the critique 'as
emancipatory knowledge' remains unattainable unless such dialogue

starts to develop.   Genuine confirmation 'can only be gained in
communication of the type of therapeutic "discourse", that is, precisely in successful processes of education voluntarily agreed to by
the recipients themselves'.   This 'negotiation of meanings', which
ethnomethodologists smugly take for the bread and butter of ordinary
routine, is in fact a rare and precious phenomenon on a social plane
higher than the realm of small group, face-to-face, intimate con-
tacts.   It has to be fought for in order to be achieved.   When it
is achieved, the process of authentication - the epistemological
corollary of emancipation - is set in motion.   With that, the critique of reality enters its 'enlightenment' stage.

   At this stage, critical theory departs from the theorist's writing
desk and sails into the open waters of popular reflection - seeking
actively to re-formulate the commonsensical assessment of historical
experience and to help imagination to break through the 'conclusiveness' of past evidence.   Sometimes, the port of destination is
clearly written into the theory, while some other parts are explicitly declared off-limit.   In other cases, however, no group is excluded a priori as a potential 'patient', on the ground that its peculiar communication disturbances are beyond remedy.   Then (as in the
case of the leading members of the Frankfurt school, disenchanted
with the therapeutic amenability of the working class) what in fact
takes place is 'the diffuse dissemination of insights individually
gained in the style of the eighteenth-century Enlightenment'.   On
the whole, there is a growing tendency among critical theorists to-
day towards the realization that, in Habermas's terse words, 'there
can be no meaningful theory which per se, and regardless of the
circumstances, obligates one to militancy'. (23)  The answer to
whether or not the distortion of communication along a specific
borderline is so grave as to eliminate the possibility of repair,
cannot be established by theoretical insight alone: it is, in fact,
one of these crucial hypotheses which can be verified only in the
course of enlightenment.   There are, in other words, no barriers to
communication which cannot be, at least in principle, dissolved.
The burden of proof that this is not the case lies with the practice
of education.

   We know already how the strategy of scientific research defines
success in terms of fact-finding and theory formulation.   Clearly,
enlightenment must have its own criteria of success, which simultaneously serve the purpose of confirming the truth of critical hypotheses.   To discover such criteria, one can again use the analogy
of psychoanalytic dialogue.   In therapy, the 'patient' must recognize himself in the interpretations offered by the therapist.   If
he does, then such interpretations are recognized by the therapist as
true.   The important distinction between this method of truth-
testing and the method applied in the first, analytical stage, is
that the hypothesis itself is active and operative in creating conditions in which it can become true.   There is little chance that
the would-be patient will ever arrive at the new interpretation entirely on his own, without a therapist, or, more generally, an external agent acting in the therapist's role, being around to offer an
interpretation distinct from the one commonsensically imposed by the
patient's situation.   And so it is the protracted negotiation of the
alternative interpretation which may eventually generate a new situ-

ation in which this interpretation 'becomes' true by having been
assimilated into the consciousness of the patient, and thereby 'authenticated'.

Similarly, in the case of re-interpreting the historical experience of a group instead of individual biographical lore, the authentication of an alternative interpretation requires the previous
active presence of a relevant hypothesis and a properly organized
process of its negotiation.   The activity of enlightenment, unlike
the truth-testing activity of science, is not aimed at discovering
that the interest it ascribes to a group is indeed the 'real interest'
of the group in question, but at attaining a situation in which that
group will actually adopt the ascribed interest as its own and 'real'.
The enlightenment process consists, therefore, in a dialogue, in
which critical theorists attempt to negotiate the alternative meanings they offer and apply persuasion to convince their partners of
their adequacy.   Whether they will succeed or not, depends, on the
whole, on the degree of correspondence between the interpretive formula contained in the critical theory and the volume of experience
collectively accumulated and commonsensically assimilated by the
group.   Such correspondence must be given the opportunity of being
carefully considered and scrupulously assessed by all the participants:  'In a process of enlightenment there can be only participants'
- and even the most spectacular success of theory in embracing human
imagination and action ought not to be taken as a proof of the truth
contained in the theory, unless the dialogue has been conducted in
conditions of unlimited intellectual freedom.   Authenticity is attainable, by definition, only in a situation of equality of the partners to the dialogue.   The sign of authentication is precisely the
former patient's emerging from his subordinate position on the re-
ceiving end of the dialogue, and assuming the role of a fully developed, creative agent of meaning-negotiation.   A dialogue conducted
in conditions of inequality of partners, or in a situation in which
contending interpretations are suppressed or made inaccessible,
proves nothing, whatever its tangible results;  it certainly cannot
lead to emancipation.   Instead, it can only substitute one type of
unfreedom for another, or one philosophical formula of unfreedom for
another.

It is clear that the authentication test, peculiar to the process
of enlightenment, lacks the elegance and the air of finality which
characterizes the truth-testing of positive science.   It is true
that the scientific method of truth testing allows far more ambiguity
than scientists would be prepared consciously to tolerate:  if an
experiment fails, there is always a possibility of at least two opposite interpretations (one of which is ineptness in the organization
of experiment), and thus the sought-after refutation of the theory,
which the experiment was designed to test, can be recognized as inconclusive and postponed.   There are, however, limits to such post-
ponement, and the method contains (at least theoretically) a proviso
which, if rigorously applied, will ward off the manifestations of
vested interests arising, say, from subjective attachment of the
theory under scrutiny.   Having placed the world it investigates in
the position of an object 'over there', and having excluded from its
preoccupations those occurrences in which the conduct of the object
may be influenced by knowledge of the scientist's intentions or

interpretations, positive science at least prevents its practitioners from defending the theories they fail to confirm by blaming the failure on the 'obtuseness' or 'collusion' of the object.   Such statements whose confirmation/refutation can be staved off by the deliberate action of the objects of research, are simply not considered as statements of positive science.   Critical knowledge, however, the moment it opts for the test of authentication, does not accept that self-limitation, and therefore lays itself open to that volume of inconclusiveness and incertitude which is hardly tolerable on the level of scientific discourse.

The price the theory which subjects itself to the test of authentication pays for pulling down the barrier dividing the 'experimenter' and his 'objects', for dissolving the difference in status between them, is likely to be considered exorbitant by a science concerned more with certainty than with the significance of its results.   In the process of enlightenment, the addressees of the theory must be endowed with the same faculties as the theoreticians themselves - above all, with the faculties of reasoning, planning, behaving in-order-to-, pursuing subjective ends, etc.   Therefore, the range of excuses which can be invoked to cast doubt on the conclusiveness of refuting evidence, is much wider here than in the discursive act of truth-testing.   One excuse, however, is similar to the major self-defence of scientific theory:  educators who fail to get their message through, may always (at least for a time) blame their lack of success on the technical imperfection of the educational process, and may try again, having rectified the genuine or alleged organizational flaws.   This is an excuse isomorphic with the argument from 'impurity of experiment', frequently applied in scientific discourse, and in its turn put to the test before the relevant theory is finally refuted.   But another excuse is peculiar to the test of authentication, inasmuch as it refers to the specific relationship between the theorist and his objects, typical of enlightenment dialogue.   In a crude form, that excuse is reasoned along the following lines:  people whose situation and prospects our theory intends to re-interpret would certainly embrace the theory and wholeheartedly approve of its arguments - were they only (i) more perceptive and open to reason, or (ii) less prone to barter away their prospects for a mess of pottage, or (iii) less completely and hopelessly stultified by their oppressors who hold their intellect to ransom.   All three variations of the argument recognize 'the people' as potentially equal partners to the dialogue;  indeed, they make sense only in the light of such recognition.   Within the assumptions of authentication, they make reasonable hypotheses which can hardly be resolutely refuted.   Nevertheless, the sheer possibility of their being invoked considerably detracts from the resolution with which the rules of refutation, specific to enlightenment dialogue, can be enforced.   Hence the intrinsic inconclusiveness of all critical theory, which makes it imperfect by much more severe scientific standards.   Hence, as well, the abstract possibility of the perpetuation of error and postponing the admission of failure indefinitely - unheard of in the field of scientific discourse.

It is all very well for Habermas to stress that processes of enlightenment:

merely support the theory's claim to truth, without valid-

ating it, as long as all those potentially involved, to
whom the theoretical interpretation has reference, have not
had the chance of accepting or rejecting the interpretation
offered under suitable circumstances . (24)

But one can easily see that it is not only the truth of the theory,
but its untruth as well which is held in suspension by the above
stipulation.   In this light particularly, the unspecified nature of
'suitable circumstances', which, only when provided, can lend finality to the outcomes of enlightenment, deprives the authentication
test of almost all exactitude and specificity and, consequently, of
an authority comparable to that of scientific truth-testing.   It
seems that this degree of indeterminacy cannot be fully eliminated
from critical knowledge, which intends to play an emancipatory role
and, consequently, embarks on the adventure of enlightenment, submitting itself to the test of authentication.   In other words, no
available code of rules can free the agent of enlightenment from
private, subjective responsibility for his interpretation of history
and the obstinacy with which he tries to render it acceptable to all.
The design of enlightenment entails, as its irremovable constituent,
the factor of courage and risk-taking.   Enlightenment is aimed not
at description and the instrumental perfection of 'human nature', but
at changing it.   The limits of such changeability can be tested only
in practical trial.   The utopian edge of culture, long remaining
'unrealistic', may suddenly start moulding human praxis when it meets
with practical necessities generated by social reality itself.   But
there is no way of knowing in advance that such an encounter is certain .   Emancipation is an effort aimed at the future, and the
future, unlike the past, is indeed inseparably the realm of freedom
for the acting man, inasmuch as it is the realm of uncertainty for
the knowing man.   The presence of the 'utopian' project is, nevertheless, a condition of its being at least possible.

However carefully selected in the first, scientific trial of truth
testing, theories emerge from the second test - that of authentication - neither conclusively confirmed nor conclusively disproved.
There is, therefore, no single, unambiguous route leading from the
second enlightenment stage, to the third - that of practical action
aimed at adjusting social reality to the newly accepted set of
meanings.   It is on this decisive threshhold where courage and the
decision to take risk become indispensable vehicles;   and, to be
sure, where the gravest and most costly mistakes can be made, more
often than not confounding the very emancipatory intent of action.
Particularly important in this context is the choice between the
continuation of the dialogue (supported by the hope that improvement
in the organization of education can increase its chance of final
success), or its termination, on the assumption that the communication has been broken definitely and beyond all chance of repair.
The crucial decision, in other words, concerns the classification of
the opposite number as a partner in the dialogue or implacable
enemy.   That is, the choice between the pragmatics of persuasion
and the pragmatics of struggle.

Once again the therapeutic analogy may help to elucidate some dimensions of the problem.   Having failed repeatedly to draw his
patient into a meaningful dialogue, the analyst is tempted to put
the blame squarely on his opposite number.   Instead of revising the

formula he has tried to negotiate, he will then define the patient's
ability to enter the dialogue as being irreparably damaged, and
classify the patient himself as incurably ill.   Under closer scrutiny, this conclusion seems to convey the analyst's failure to obtain
communication, rather than any objective attributes of the patient
himself.   This conclusion makes sense only as the summing-up of a
series of repetitive, but abortive attempts to start a dialogue and
to force the partner into acceptance of the formula considered by the
analyst to be true.   Since, however, any dialogue can confirm or
disprove the discussed formula only tentatively - no dialogue, whatever its course, contains conclusive proof that the decision of the
analyst to terminate communication was 'true';   that, in other words,
it indeed rightly reflected certain 'objective' qualities of the
patient.

   In practice, the decision of an ideologically committed group to
declare another group as organically closed to communication and to
classify it as a case in which limitation of freedom by force is
justified, is even less controlled by the formal requirements of
verification than the decision of the analyst to confine his prosp-
ective partner to the mental hospital.   Groups engaged in the process of enlightenment do not enjoy the greenhouse conditions of pure
dialogue, neither can they invoke the special authority granted to
them by established institutions or commonsense.   Even if able to
control the rationality of their own conduct and judgment, they would
find it practically impossible to accept the evidence of their
failure as final.   Once taken, their decision to blame the obstinate
partner for the breakdown of the dialogue and to declare him 'incurably ill', will act as a self-fulfilling prophecy, thereby lending
a spurious air of veracity to a rule-of-the-thumb verdict.   Indeed,
once placed outside the dialogue, in a subordinate and unfree position, the condemned group will never be able to engage in dialogue.
In view of the seriousness of the danger, one has to emphasize as
strongly as possible that, whatever the course of the dialogue, it
will never supply conclusive evidence for a hypothesis that one of
its partners is inherently unable to embrace the truth and that,
therefore, struggle is the only rational and viable attitude.   We
know only too well how often this vital fact tends to be forgotten in
politics and how disastrous the results of forgetting it might be.

   In the absence of rules which can guide decisions taken on this
threshold  with anything approaching algorythmical exactitude, one
has to settle for more lenient and equivocal heuristic guidelines.
These can go only in the direction of shared responsibility and the
creation of conditions where - one would hope - the guidance of human
action by reason will be unimpaired.   This general direction has
been selected on the assumption, that given real freedom to exercise
their judgment and reflect on all aspects of their situation, men
will eventually make the right choice between alternative interpretations;   or, to put it in a somewhat more cautious form - the freer
the conditions of judgment, the higher is the probability that true
interpretations are adopted and false rejected.   Hence, at each
stage of the long process of verification of critical knowledge,
proper care is to be taken in eliminating intellectual and physical
constraints upon judgment.   At the level of theoretical discourse,
all information, and the procedure of testing it, must be open to

general scrutiny and all criticism carefully considered before the
assumption of its validity.   At the stage of enlightenment dialogue,
all necessary effort must be made to lift all participants to the
status of full intellectual partners in communication, and to avoid
interference of non-intellectual means in the clash between competing
interpretations.   Finally, if a decision has been taken to enter a
third stage - that of struggle - on the assumption that the communication with some group has been irreparably broken, all decisions
must be made again dependent upon the consent of all participants,
preceded by thorough and uncurbed scanning of alternative means of
action.   These heuristic guidelines are, in effect, exemplificat-
ions of the general principle:  the liberation of man can be promoted
only in conditions of liberty.   The concept of critical knowledge
serving the emancipatory interest of man cannot but agree with the
seminal principle and the intellectual 'spiritus movens' of the
Enlightenment:  that the emancipation of reason is a condition of
all material emancipation.

Those who seek knowledge of the kind whose veracity one can be
fully certain of at the moment one formulates it, will obtain little
comfort from such vague heuristic guidelines for authentication as
the self-reflection of critical knowledge can offer.   But, then,
the one thing men can be certain of, more than of anything else, is
that they have never, so far, attained the kind of freedom they
sought.   And freedom means uncertainty as much as certitude means
resignation.   But before he may be a thinker, a symbol-maker, a
homo faber - man has to be he-who-hopes.

# NOTES

CHAPTER 1   THE SCIENCE OF UNFREEDOM

1  Cf. Gerald Holton, 'The Thematic Origins of Scientific Thought', Harvard University Press, 1973, pp.35-6.
2  Karl Marx, 'Grundrisse', Penguin (Pelican), 1973, p.489.   Translated by Martin Nicolaus.
3  Ibid., p.157.
4  Herbert Marcuse, Industrialization and Capitalism, in 'Max Weber and Sociology Today', ed. Otto Stammer, Basil Blackwell, Oxford, 1971, p.145.
5  Peter Gay, 'The Enlightenment, An Interpretation', vol.1, 'The Rise of Modern Paganism', Wildwood House, London, 1970, p.148.
6  Emile Durkheim, 'Socialism and Saint-Simon', Routledge & Kegan Paul, London, 1959, p.113.   Translated by Charlotte Sattler.
7  'The Crisis of Industrial Civilization, the early essays of Auguste Comte', Introduced by Ronald Fletcher, Heinemann, London, 1974, p.28.
8  Quoted from 'Essential Comte', ed. S. Andreski, Croom Helm, London, 1974, pp.159, 176.   Translated by Margaret Clarke.
9  Quoted from 'The Crisis ...', op.cit. p.80.
10  Ibid., pp.211, 80, 78.
11  'Social Contract, Locke, Hume, and Rousseau', Oxford University Press, 1966, p.290.
12  Emile Durkheim, 'Sociology and Philosophy', Cohen & West, London, 1965, pp.51-2.   Translated by  D.F. Pocock.
13  Ibid., pp.57, 72.
14  Pascal, 'Pensées', Penguin, 1966, pp.66, 65, 137, 136.   Translated by A.J. Krailsheimer.
15  Durkheim, 'Sociology and Philosophy', p.55.
16  Emile Durkheim, 'The Elementary Forms of the Religious Life', Allen & Unwin, London, 1968, pp.422-3.   Translated by J.W. Swain.
17  Ibid., pp.436, 419.
18  Culture, Personality, and Society, in 'Anthropology Today', ed. Sol Tax, University of Chicago Press, 1962, p.365.
19  Psychoanalytic Characterology, in 'Culture and Personality', ed. S.S. Sargeant and W.M. Smith, New York, 1949, p.10.
20  Cf. General Theory in Sociology, in 'Sociology Today', ed.

Robert K. Merton et al., Basic Books, New York, 1959.
21 'Toward a General Theory of Action', ed. Talcott Parsons and Edward A. Shils, Harper & Row, New York, 1962, p.16.
22 Manfred Stanley, The Structures of Doubt, in 'Toward the Sociology of Knowledge', ed. Gunther W. Remmling, Routledge & Kegan Paul, London, 1973, p.430.
23 Erving Goffman, On Face Work, in 'Interation Ritual', Penguin, 1967, pp.42-3.
24 Erwing Goffman, 'The Presentation of Self in Everyday Life', Doubleday, 1959, p.3.
25 As recently Barry Hindess, with an ardour worthy of a Skinner, demonstrated in his review of Dahrendorf's 'Homo Sociologicus' - THES N.143, 12 July 1974.
26 Rollo May, in 'Existential Psychology', ed. Rollo May, Random House, New York, 1969, p.90.
27 Soeren Kierkegaard, 'The Concept of Dread', Princeton University Press, 1944, p.55. Translated by Walter Lowrie.
28 Leszek Kolakowski, Obecnosc Mitu, Instytut Literacki, Paris, 1972, p.29.
29 Cf. 'An Augustine Synthesis', ed. G.E. Przywara, New York, 1958, p.75.
30 Jurgen Habermas, 'Theory and Practice', Heinemann, London, 1974, p.8. Translated by John Viertel.
31 From the Positive Philosophy. Quoted from the 'Classical Statements', ed. Marcello Truzzi, Random House, New York, 1971, pp.40-41.
32 Bernard Berelson, 'Introduction to the Behavioural Sciences', Voice of America Forum Lectures, Behavioural Sciences Series, p.2.
33 George Lundberg, The Future of the Social Sciences, 'Scientific Monthly', October 1941.
34 B.F. Skinner, The Scheme of Behaviour Explanation, in 'Philosophical Problems of the Social Sciences', ed. David Braybrooke, Macmillan, 1965, p.44.
35 B.F. Skinner, Is a Science of Human Behaviour Possible?, in ibid., pp.24-5.

## CHAPTER 2  CRITIQUE OF SOCIOLOGY

1 Robert Heilbroner, Through the Marxian Maze, 'The New York Review of Books', vol.18, N.4.
2 Quoted from Gordon Leff, 'Medieval Thought', Penguin, 1970, p.39.
3 For Husserl's desperate attempt to demonstrate the compatibility of phenomenology with the sociological problem, see the excellent study by René Toulemont, 'L'Essence de la société selon Husserl', Presses Universitaires de France, 1962.
4 Erwin Laszlo, 'Beyond Scepticism and Realism', Martinus Nijhoff, The Hague, 1966, p.222.
5 Cf. Alfred Schutz in 'Reflections on the Problem of Relevance', ed. Richard M. Zaner, Yale University Press, New Haven, 1970, p.43.
6 Cf. Alfred Schutz and Thomas Luckmann, 'The Structures of the Life World', Heinemann, London, 1974, p.271f. Translated by Richard M. Zaner and M. Tristram Engelhardt, Jr.
7 Cf. Anselm L. Strauss, 'Mirrors and Masks, The Search for Identity', Free Press, New York, 1959, p.91f.

8  Maurice Natanson, 'The Social Dynamics of George H. Mead',
Introduction by Horace M. Kallen, Martinus Nijhoff, The Hague, 1973,
p.vii.
9  Peter L. Berger and Thomas Luckmann, 'The Social Construction of
Reality', Penguin, 1967.
10  Ibid., pp.177-8.


CHAPTER 3  CRITIQUE OF UNFREEDOM


1  Jurgen Habermas, 'Theory and Practice', Heinemann, London, 1974,
p.256 ff.    Translated by John Viertel.
2  Peter L. Berger, Identity as a Problem in the Sociology of Knowledge, in 'Towards the Sociology of Knowledge', ed. Gunter W. Remmling, Routledge & Kegan Paul, London, 1973, pp.275-6.
3  Henry S. Kariel, 'Open Systems', F.E. Peacock, Itasca, Ill.,
1971, p.86.
4  Habermas, op.cit., pp.275-6.
5  John R. Seeley, Thirty Nine Articles:  Toward a Theory of Social
Theory, in 'The Critical Spirit, Essays in Honour of Herbert Marcuse',
ed. Kurt H. Wolff and Barrington Moore, Jr., Beacon Press, Boston,
1967, pp.168-9.
6  Karl Marx, 'Grundrisse', Penguin, 1973, p.156 ff.    Translated by
Martin Nicolaus.
7  Ibid., pp.162-3.
8  Ibid., p.162.
9  Ibid., p.164.
10  Habermas, op.cit., p.261.
11  Max Horkheimer, Materialismus und Moral, in 'Kritische Theorie',
ed. Alfred Schmidt, vol.I, Frankfurt-am-Main, p.85.
12  Manfred Stanley, The Structures of Doubt, in 'Toward the Sociology of Knowledge', ed. Remmling, op.cit., p.419.
13  Quoted after David McLellan, 'The Thought of Karl Marx', Macmillan, London, 1971, p.33.
14  Marx, op.cit., p.461-3.
15  Edgar Morin, Pour une sociologie de la crise, 'Communications',
Paris, 1968, 12, pp.2-16.
16  Henry S. Kariel, Expanding the Political Present, 'American Political Science Review', September 1969.
17  Stanford M. Lyman and Marvin B. Scott, 'A Sociology of the Absurd',
Appleton-Century-Crofts, New York, 1970, p.16.
18  Stanley, op.cit.
19  Ernst Bloch, 'On Marx', Herder and Herder, New York, 1971, p.41.
Translated by John Maxwell.
20  Ibid., pp.98-100.
21  Habermas, op.cit., p.21 ff.
22  Ibid., p.25 ff.
23  Ibid., p.32 ff.
24  Ibid., p.37-8.